Such is the lan-
guage of a beaft-
ly railor,
The Divels privi-
houfe moft fit
for *Taylor*.

We are each our own devil, and we
make this world our hell.
Oscar Wilde

My own thoughts were that much good might have come if the case had been reported, and people had come to realize that the presence and activity of the Devil is something very real... and possibly never more real than at the present time. I can assure you of one thing: The case in which I was involved with the real thing. I had no doubt about it then and I have no doubt about it now.
Father William Bowdern

Personally, I do not believe that Rob Doe was possessed. There is simply too much evidence that indicates that as a boy he had serious emotional problems stemming from his home life. There is not one shred of hard evidence to support the notion of demonic possession.
Mark Opsasnick

I have no idea what was really going on in that hospital room but I can tell you that the things that I heard coming from behind that door scared the hell out of me!
A Former Employee of the Alexian Brothers Hospital

THE DEVIL CAME TO ST. LOUIS

The True Story of the 1949 Exorcism

TROY TAYLOR

Abraham Lincoln once spoke of the "better angels of our natures" and if we believe that such "better angels" exist, then we must believe that those angels have an opposite number in the darkest corner of our hearts. This book is for those who keep such darker angels at bay.

Original Cover Artwork Designed by
© Copyright 2014 by April Slaughter & Troy Taylor
Back Cover Author's Photo by Janet Morris

This Book is Published By:
Whitechapel Press
A Division of Apartment 42 Productions
Decatur, Illinois   1-888-GHOSTLY
Visit us on the internet at http: www.whitechapelpress.com

Second Edition - January 2014
ISBN: 1-892523-46-9

Printed in the United States of America

FOREWORD

In 1949, the Devil came to St. Louis.....

Or at least, if you believe the stories that have been told for the last sixty-odd years, a reasonable facsimile of him did.

From the August 20, 1949 edition of the *Washington Post*:

In what is perhaps one of the most remarkable experiences of its kind in recent religious history, a 14 year-old Mount Rainier boy has been freed by a Catholic priest of possession by the devil, it was reported yesterday.

Only after 20 to 30 performances of the ancient ritual of exorcism, here and in St. Louis, was the devil finally cast out of the boy, it was said.

In all except the last of these, the boy broke into a violent tantrum of screaming, cursing and voicing of Latin phrases --- a language he had never studied --- whenever the priest reached those climactic points of the 27-page ritual in which he commanded the demon to depart from the boy.

In complete devotion to his task the priest stayed with the boy over a period of two months, during which he witnessed such manifestations as the bed in which the boy was sleeping suddenly moving across the room.

A Washington Protestant minister has previously reported personally witnessing similar manifestations, including one in which the pallet on which the sleeping boy lay slid slowly across the floor until the boy's head bumped against a bed, awakening him.

In another instance reported by the Protestant minister, a heavy armchair in which the boy was sitting, with his knees drawn under his chin, tilted slowly to one side and fell over, throwing the boy on the floor.

The final rite of exorcism in which the devil was cast from the boy took place in May, it was reported, and since then he had had no manifestations. The ritual in its present form goes back 1,500 years and from there to Jesus Christ. But before it was undertaken, all medical and psychiatric means of curing the boy ---- in whose presence such manifestations as fruit jumping up from the refrigerator top in his home and hurling itself against the wall also were reported --- were exhausted.

The boy was taken to Georgetown University Hospital here, where his affliction was exhaustively studied, and to St. Louis University. Both are Jesuit institutions. Finally both Catholic hospitals reported they were unable to cure the boy through natural means. Only then was a supernatural cure sought.

The ritual was undertaken by a Jesuit in his 50's. The details of the exorcism of the boy were described to the Washington Post by a priest here not the exorcist . The ritual began in St. Louis, continued here and finally ended in St. Louis.

For two months, the Jesuit stayed with the boy, accompanying him back and forth on the train, sleeping in the same house and sometimes in the same room with him. He witnessed many of the same manifestations reported by the Protestant minister this month to a closed meeting of the Society of Parapsychology laboratory at Duke University, who came here to study the case, was quoted as saying it was "the most impressive" poltergeist noisy ghost phenomenon that had come to his attention in his years of celebrated investigation in the field.

Even through the ritual of exorcism the boy was by no means cured readily. The ritual itself takes about three quarters of an hour to perform. During it, the boy would break into the fury of profanity and screaming and the astounding Latin phrases.

But finally, at the last performance of the ritual, the boy was quiet. And since then, it was said, all manifestations of the affliction --- such as the strange moving of the bed across the room, and another in which the boy's family said a picture had suddenly jutted out from the wall in his presence --- have ceased.

It was early this year that members of the boy's family went to their minister and reported strange goings-on in their Mount Rainier house since January 18. The minister visited the boy's home and witnessed some of the manifestations. But though they seemed to the naked eye unexplainable --- such as the scratchings from the area of the wall in the boy's presence ---- there was always

6

the suggestion, he said, that in some way the noises may have been made by the boy himself.

Retaining his skepticism in the matter, the minister than had the boy stay a night --- February 17 --- in his own home. It was there, before his own eyes, he said, that the two manifestations that he felt were beyond all natural explanation took place. In one of these the boy's pallet moved across the floor while his hands were outside the cover and his body rigid. In the other, the heavy chair, with the boy immobile in it, tilted and fell over to the floor before the minister's amazed eyes, he said. The minister tried to overturn the chair while sitting in it himself and was unable to do so.

The case involved such reactions as neighbors of the boy's family sprinkling holy water around the family's house.

Some of the Mount Rainier neighbors' skepticism was startlingly resolved, it was reported, when they first laughed it off, invited the boy and his mother to spend the night in their own "unhaunted" homes, only to have some of the manifestations --- such as the violent, apparently involuntary shakings of the boy's bed --- happen before their eyes.

This article is a brief synopsis of a story that has been told for almost four generations and one that has inspired books, films and documentaries. It is, without question, the greatest unsolved mystery of the city of St. Louis and one of the most perplexing puzzles of the supernatural in American history. But is the story so mysterious because of the events that occurred --- or because of the bizarre mixture of fact and fantasy that it has become? The story of the 1949 St. Louis Exorcism has become a confusing and convoluted mess over the years. There are so many theories, legends, tales and counter-stories that have been thrown into the mix that it's become very hard to separate just what is truth and what is fiction in the case.

When I wrote the original edition of this book back in 2006, my intent was to separate the truth from the fiction. What part of the story, that so many of us have come to know, is nothing more than just the result of wild imagination --- and what part of it really took place? Can we really get to the bottom of what happened in 1949, despite all of the unanswered questions that have been left behind? What really happened in Maryland that would drive a family halfway across the country to look for answers? And what happened at the old Alexian Brothers hospital that still has former staff members whispering about it in fear? And most of all, was this boy really possessed by a demon?

I was never able to promise that I would accomplish all of that. However, I do believe that I succeeded in my real goal: to provide enough evidence for the reader to judge for himself or herself what they chose to believe - or not believe

7

- about the case. I never set out to decide the truthfulness of the story. I wanted the reader to decide that they believed. I knew what I believed about the case - or at least I thought I did at the time. Since 2006, though, I have changed my mind about some of the elements of what did, or did not, happen. And most certainly about what I believe has happened since 1949...

It is a very strange journey that we will embark upon in the pages ahead. The history of exorcism dates back several centuries, but the tale of what happened in St. Louis takes us to the middle part of the last century and continues into the present day. The story of the St. Louis Exorcism did not end in 1949. In fact, its presence is still being felt today.

What effect will this story have on you, as the reader? If you are like me, it's liable to have you reading this book with the lights on. Supernatural or not, *something* happened to a young Maryland boy in 1949 and we can't help but wonder if it happened to him, could it happen to someone we know?

Could it happen to us?

That's something to think about as you turn the pages of this book. What lurks in the outer reaches of the supernatural? What lurks in the back of our own minds? Prepare to be disturbed by what you are about to read. Prepare to be frightened. You may tell yourself that this is only a book --- but remember, this story is true and what happened in St. Louis can happen anywhere. You can tell yourself that you don't believe that people can be possessed by supernatural beings but what you believe may not matter.

You may not believe in them --- but they believe in you.

Spooky, huh?

Who knows? This may be nothing more, as some people claim, than the story of a boy who "created" a demon as an excuse for bad behavior and a reason not to attend school. Could this really be the case? Again, I can't say for sure but you can certainly keep telling yourself that every time you have the urge to look back over your shoulder while you are reading this book.

And you will have the urge to look ---- and I'll bet you keep the light on as well.

Troy Taylor
Winter 2014

INTRODUCTION

THE HISTORY & MYSTERY OF EXORCISMS

In 1865, something horrific and beyond explanation entered the lives of two young boys in the small town of Illfurth, in Alsace, France. The boys, Joseph and Theobald Bruner, eight- and ten-years old, were the sons of a local farmer and lived a quiet and ordinary existence. According to records kept by their parish priest, Father Karl Brey, the first indication that something was seriously wrong with the children came with a newfound fascination with diabolic things and a sudden aversion to anything of a religious nature. He wrote:

While lying in their bed, the children used to turn to the wall, paint horrible Devil faces on it, and then speak to the faces and play with them. If, while one of the possessed was asleep, a rosary was placed on his bed, he would immediately hide under the covers and refuse to come out of hiding until the rosary was removed.

Soon, things took a more serious turn as the children began to undergo terrifying physical contortions. Father Brey recalled:

They entangled their legs every two or three hours in an unnatural way. They knotted so intricately that it was impossible to pull them apart. And yet, suddenly, they could untangle them with lightning speed. At times the boys stood simultaneously on their heads and legs, bent backwards, their bodies arched high.

9

No amount of outside pressure could bring their bodies into a normal position --
-- until the Devil saw fit to give these objects of his torture some temporary
peace.

Father Brey was quickly convinced that the boys were possessed and his
diary recorded more strange happenings:

At times, their bodies became bloated as if about to burst; when this happened,
the boy would vomit. Whereby yellow foam, feathers and seaweed would come
out of his mouth. Often their clothes were covered with evil smelling feathers....
No matter how often their shirts and outer clothing were changed, new feathers
and seaweed would appear. These feathers, which covered their bodies in an
inexplicable way, filled the air with such a stench that they had to be burned...

The priest also recounted other seemingly supernatural indications that the
boys were diabolically possessed. He was especially impressed by Joseph and
Theobald's frequent displays of clairvoyance:

Theobald several times predicted the death of a person correctly. Two hours
before the death of a Fran Muller, the boy knelt by his bed and acted as if he
were ringing a mourning bell. Another time he did the same thing for a whole
hour. When he was asked for whom he was ringing, the boy answered, "For
Gregor Kunegel." As it happened, Kunegel's daughter was visiting in the house.
Shocked and angry, she told Theobald, "You liar, my father is not even ill. He is
working on the new boy's seminary building as a mason." Theobald answered.
"That may be, be he just had a fall. Go ahead and check on it!" The facts bore
him out. The man had fallen from a scaffold, breaking his neck. This happened
at the very moment that Theobald made the bell-ringing motions. No one in
Illfurth had been aware of the accident.

When Father Brey, and the boys' parents, decided that an exorcism was the
only way to help them, Theobald was sent to the St. Charles Orphanage at
Schiltigheim near Strasbourg. The orphanage was run by nuns and its superior
was a Father Stumpf. For the first three days after his arrival, Theobald --- or
the demonic entity --- was silent but on the fourth day he spoke. "I have come
and I am in a rage," the voice declared. One of the nuns asked him who he was
and what they described as a "nonhuman voice" loudly answered, "I am the Lord
of Darkness."

A short time later, Joseph was also sent to the orphanage and the rites of
exorcism began. During the prolonged period that followed, the exorcism was

carried out by Father Stumpf and the possession of the two brothers manifested itself in many ways. For instance, both boys became infested with red head lice, which multiplied so quickly that three or four nuns with brushes and combs were unable to keep pace with them. Eventually, the priest poured holy water on the vermin and they disappeared.

In all, the possession of Theobald and Joseph Bruner lasted more than four years. They were freed by the rite of exorcism but tragically, Theobald died two years later, in April 1871, when he was sixteen. Joseph, whose symptoms had been less severe, lived only a few years longer. He died in 1882, still a young man.

The possession - or at least the exorcisms they were subjected to - destroyed the lives of the two young boys and unquestionably led to their deaths.

EXORCISMS IN HISTORY

We've all seen the movie. We all think we know what happens when someone is possessed. But do we really? Heads spin around, furniture and people levitate, pea soup is vomited all over the room --- pretty scary and nasty stuff. But is any of this real or is this stuff merely the created from the imaginations of novelists and screenwriters?

And most importantly, are people really possessed?

The state of "possession" had been defined as the presence of a spirit or entity that occupies and controls the physical body of the subject. Belief in this phenomenon has long existed in most countries of the world and in the Christian religion, it was once regarded as the exclusive domain of demons acting in the interest of Satan. This belief comes from a number of references in the Bible, including a passage from Mark that states, "In my name shall they cast out devils"; from Luke that reads, "Then he called his twelve disciples together and gave them power and authority over all devils"; and also from Luke, "And the seventy returned again with joy, saying Lord, even the devils are subject unto us through Thy name." There is also the story of when Jesus confronts a man who is possessed by so many demons that they call themselves "Legion." He exorcizes the spirits and banishes them into a herd of pigs, who commit mass suicide by throwing themselves off a cliff. Thanks to references such as these, demonic possession remains a tenet of the Christian church, especially of the Roman Catholic faith.

But possession, as such, has many faces. The symptoms can include agonized convulsions, often with writhing and posturing of sexual desire, the mouthing of obscenities, vomiting, reports of poltergeist-like happenings, terrible violence and even a state of unnatural calm. No unanimous opinion exists today as to the causes, or causes, of possession and the subject has involved such varied disciplines as religion, medicine, psychiatry, spiritualism and demonology. As in most cases of possible supernatural behavior, the possibility of fraud cannot be overlooked and many cases that were once thought to be genuine have later been questioned or disproved. However, it is clear that in many cases, the symptoms, sometimes of deep distress, mental or even physical torment, are genuine, no matter how controversial the cause. This does not dismiss the possibility that the symptoms of the possession may be the result of suggestion, external or self-induced, and that victims may be better served by the care of a psychiatrist rather than an exorcist.

As far as most doctors and mental health specialists are concerned, the diagnosis of demonic possession is one that reeks of medieval superstition and ignorance. The symptoms, they believe, are subject to either a wide range of medical and psychiatric interpretations or can be dismissed as misperceptions and hallucinations. They feel that the cases of possession in the past were nothing more than conditions like epilepsy, hysteria or what has been referred to as multiple personality disorder, which is rare in itself.

During a convulsive seizure, a person with epilepsy can experience extreme muscular rigidity, foaming at the mouth and rapid back and forth head movements. Their face may be distorted and they may produce strange, guttural noises that are caused by a spasm of the throat muscles. During the period just before a seizure, the patient may experience hallucinations, seeing things and hearing weird sounds and voices.

According to all of the literature of possession, these are also symptoms of being possessed. But there are differences. Demonic attacks allegedly lasted for hours at a time, not just the five minutes or so attributed to epileptic seizures. Extreme movements, rather than rigidity, are more characteristic to a possessed person and muscular reflexes tend to be strong. According to church records, other signs of a possession include "the ability to speak with some familiarity in a strange tongue or to understand it when spoken by another; the faculty of divulging future and hidden events; and the display of powers which are beyond the subject's age and natural condition."

A condition called hysteria also produces many of the symptoms of someone who is possessed. The following description of a female hysteric was recorded in the early 1900s by Professor Paul Richter, a French doctor at La Salpetriere, a famous mental hospital in Paris:

Suddenly, we heard loud cries and shouting. Her body, which went through a series of elaborate motions, was either in the throes of wild gyrations or catatonically motionless. Her legs became entangled, then disentangled, her arms twisted and disjointed, her wrists bent. Some of her fingers were stretched out straight, while others were twisted. Her body was either bent in a semi-circle or loose-limbed. Her head was at times thrown to the right or left or, when thrown backward with vehemence, seemed to emerge from a bloated neck. The face alternately mirrored horror, anger and sometimes fury; it was bloated and showed shades of violet in its coloration....

Two of the most striking details in Richter's writings are the description of the woman's entangling and disentangling legs and that of her body "bent in a semi-circle." The notation about her legs brings to mind the descriptions of the Bruner boys in the 1865 case that was mentioned in the beginning of this chapter. The description of what is referred to as the "hysterical arch" in some texts is frequently seen in cases of possession. All of the other symptoms described above have also been observed by exorcists over the years. In addition, the appearance

13

of livid marks on the skin -- sometimes resembling bites, symbols or even letters -- is also documented to be produced by hysterics.

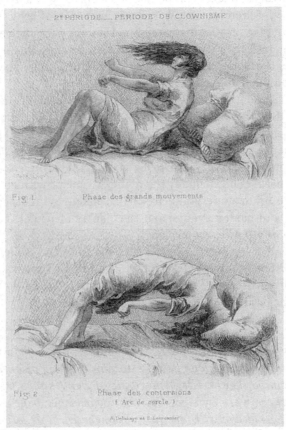

Illustrations from Richter's work, depicting the violent throes of hysterics, which might have been often mistaken for possession.

Given this partial duplication of symptoms, how does the church distinguish between hysteria and genuine cases of possession? The determining factor is the context in which the symptoms occur. If they come about at the same time as an aversion to religious objects, and if they are accompanied by paranormal phenomena the ability to detect religious items that have been hidden, understand languages never learned, levitation, and so on , the church is much more likely to consider the symptoms to be manifestations of possession.

As mysterious as hysteria, and as likely to be confused with possession, is multiple personality disorder, in which a person can manifest several different personalities. Each personality may have its own likes, dislikes and speech patterns, and may be opposed to the others or indifferent of them. If one, or more, of them seems diabolical in nature, it's possible that the disorder could be mistaken for possession. It should be noted, however, that true cases of multiple personality disorder are extremely rare. They are usually connected to repressed memories of traumatic events, such as sexual molestation, and often emerge to protect the victim from facing what happened to them. For this reason, labeling cases of possible possession as multiple personality disorder can be problematic at best.

Even so, doctors are usually violently opposed to even considering the idea of demonic possession when something medical or psychiatric might explain the symptoms being exhibited by a patient. With only a hatred of religious objects and instances of paranormal phenomena which most of them do not believe in anyway standing as the criteria for a case to be a true possession rather than hysteria, most doctors and psychiatrists are likely to reject these criteria as misperceptions and hallucinations on the part of the witness. A few, less skeptical medical professionals might concede that something strange can be going on in a case but they will probably steer toward parapsychology rather than possession.

In cases where objects are reported to move about, many will point toward poltergeist phenomena rather than the work of demonic spirits. The word "poltergeist" actually means "noisy ghost" when translated from German and for many years, researchers believed that these noisy ghosts were causing the phenomena reported in haunted house cases of a violent and destructive nature. The variety of activity connected with such cases can include knocking and pounding sounds, disturbance of stationary objects, doors slamming shut and usually violent, physical actions by sometimes heavy objects. Despite what some believe, many cases like this have nothing to do with ghosts -- or with demons either.

The most widely accepted theory in many "poltergeist-like" cases is that the activity is not caused by a ghost, but by a person in the household. This person is usually but not always an adolescent girl, and normally one who is troubled emotionally. It is thought that she is unconsciously manipulating the items in the house by "psychokinesis," the power to move things using energy generated in the mind. It is unknown why this ability seems to appear in females around the age of puberty but it has been documented to occur. Most of these disturbances are short-lived because the conditions that cause them to occur often pass quickly. The living person, or "agent" as they are called, subconsciously vents their repressed anger or frustration in way that science has yet to explain. An

15

emotionally disturbed young person might exhibit symptoms of this type, which matches some of the criteria of a possession but again, is something else entirely.

As the reader has undoubtedly discovered by now, modern science is quick to try and explain away the idea of spiritual or demonic possession. There are many possible explanations as to why a person *cannot* be possessed and yet, with each of the explanations, none of them contains all of the symptoms that a possessed person is alleged to exhibit. Does this mean that possession can be real -- or is simply that science has not yet found a reason as to why some so-called "possessions" defy explanation?

One thing is certain, whether possession is real or not, there are people all over the world who believe that it is real -- and they have whole-heartedly believed this for centuries. The belief in possession dates back to the years of the early Catholic Church but it gained prominence due to a number of famous cases during the Middle Ages. Instances of nuns possessed by satanic influences affected convents in France, Italy, Spain, Germany and elsewhere. Commonly beginning with a single nun, the possessed proved to be highly contagious and whole groups became involved. Coinciding with the relentless years of the Spanish Inquisition, the cases often had tragic consequences for anyone who might be accused of causing a person to become possessed. Usually the victims themselves were not considered to be responsible for what had occurred to them and their treatment was confined to the expulsion of the demons by exorcism. The exorcists, who formed one of the minor orders of the Church, were priests who specialized in the work using methods that had been drawn out in the *Rituale Romanum*.

The *Rituale Romanum*, which is still used in the Roman Catholic Church today, was issued in 1614 at the behest of Pope Paul V. It was designed to formalize practices that had developed during the early days of the Christian Church and it placed special emphasis on identifying diabolical possession, selection of the exorcist and defining the setting and texts to be used during an exorcism ritual. The ritual has retained its central features over the past centuries, although recent revisions were made in 1952 and 1999. The text is initially designed to establish the actual presence of demonic possession. For this, the text specifies:

First of all, one should not easily assume that someone is possessed by a demon unless he shows signs that distinguish the possessed person from those who suffer from melancholy (mental illness or some (physical) disease. The signs indicating the presence of a possessed person are as follows: speaking in an unknown tongue or understanding someone who speaks in a language unknown to the person; revelation of distant and unknown matters;

16

manifestation of powers beyond one's natural age and condition; as well as other
such matters, all of which, when taken together, compound such indications.

An early copy of the *Rituale Romanum*

However, as noted earlier and as noted by Monsignor Carlo Balducci in 1959, parapsychology has widened the possibility of natural phenomena such as psychokinesis and precognition being interpreted as demonic in origin. Combine that with mental illness and medical conditions and it becomes much harder to determine what is a real possession and what is not. For this reason, the exorcist's first task was to confirm that the victim was indeed possessed by a Christian devil, who existed only by the permission of God. In that way, the demon was subject to the authority of the Christian priest. Numerous manuals covered not only the discovery and expulsion of demons from human and animal bodies but many techniques for countering demonic offenses, both small and large. There was, it was believed in the past, scarcely any evil that a demon was not

17

capable of, from the drying up of milk cows to the more serious grievance of inhibiting the sexual intercourse of married couples.

Once a satanic origin was established, the exorcist's next problem was to find the manner of the demon's entry into the possessed, which might be due to the demon's own initiative, invitation by the possessed person or, as believed in past centuries, by the incantations of a witch. The latter was usually preferred because it meant an easier expulsion and when the witch was discovered, she could be tried, hanged or burned. The most difficult process of discovery involved situations when there seemed to be no clear reason for the victim to become possessed. In many historic cases, pious and religious people were often reportedly possessed by demons. In these cases, it was often believed that the possessions occurred as a test to the victim or even a test for the exorcist himself.

From the records, it is clear that an exorcism had the nature of a contest between the exorcist, armed with the authority of God and the Church, and the demonic intruder. An exorcist could fail. He could even be killed if the battle went against him and the fact that several exorcists died prematurely -- and several went insane -- seems to lend credence to the horror of the exorcism itself. The prayers, adjurations and commands of the exorcist, along with the ritual acts prescribed, were in themselves dramatic and when they provoked, as they were intended to do, a dialogue between the exorcist and the demon, they could be overwhelming and fantastic. For it was here that the drama of the confrontation reached its height as the demon's bestial voice belched out its obscenities and the priest's voice answered with commands and prayers.

While we think of an exorcism as "driving out" the demon, it is really more of a case of placing the demon under an oath. In some instances, there may be more than one demon possessing a person. The word "exorcism" is derived from the Greek "ek" with the verb "horkizo", which means "I cause ffisomeoneffl to swear" and refers to "putting the spirit or demon on oath." To put it simply, it means invoking a higher authority to bind the entity in order to control it and command it to act contrary to its own will. In the Christian sense, this higher authority is Jesus Christ, based on the belief that demons and evil spirits are afraid of Christ. This belief hearkens back to the story mentioned earlier when Jesus cast out a legion of devils from an afflicted man. And not only did Christ exorcize demons and unclean spirits but he gave the power to his disciples as well. "....He gave the power against unclean spirits, to cast them out, and to heal all manners of sickness, and all manner of disease." Book of Matthew

Thanks to passages in the Bible that mention the expulsion of demons, Catholics and Protestants alike believe they have the power to cast out devils and to heal the sick. The Catholic Church uses the *Rituale Romanum* as an outline for exorcisms but the ritual may vary as determined by the exorcist performing

18

the expulsion. The code of Canon Law allows authorized ministers exorcists to perform solemn exorcisms over not only the faithful but also over non-Catholics and those who have been excommunicated from the church.

The greatest danger to the exorcist during the ritual is becoming possessed by the demon himself. This is the reason why the exorcist must be as free from sin as possible and to feel no secret need for punishment. Many priests will fast and pray for some time before taking part in the ritual and during a prolonged exorcism, while they continue to fast, some will report extreme weight loss. Only a priest who is convinced that he is right with God can be safe during an exorcism. Otherwise, the demon can easily entrap him.

It is also thought that those who are physically exhausted, or in poor health, can be more easily manipulated by the demon. This is probably the reason that Malachi Martin, a former Jesuit professor, stated in his book *Hostage to the Devil* 1976 that much of the success of the exorcism depends on the exorcist. He describes the type of priest best suited to be an exorcist as a man of good physical health, being of middle age and one who has gone routinely about his pastoral duties. He is usually not a man who is considered to be brilliant or one who was engaged in teaching or research. Although, Martin adds, there are exceptions to all of these characteristics.

The *Rituale Romanum* has its own special qualifications for the priest who served as an exorcist. The qualifications were laid out in the following points:

1. He must have led a genuinely religious and virtuous life.
2. He must adhere to the rules and regulations governing exorcism, as defined by the Bishop of his diocese.
3. He must have a profound knowledge of the theory and practice of exorcism.
4. He must have a critical approach that does not yield quickly to a belief in possession.
5. In case possession exists, it is necessary to keep in mind that there are demonic beings, and low-level discarnate masters of the lie, so that every utterance of an entity must be viewed with critical detachment.
6. The exorcist must never enter the purely medical area.
7. The patient must be advised of the cautions listed above.
8. The location and manner of exorcism must be selected in accordance with faith and human dignity. For this reason, there must be no undignified behavior, no chitchat with the entity, nothing that amounts to merely questioning or inquiries into future events.

Although Martin noted that there were exceptions to the criteria that he listed for an "ideal" exorcist, he did state that he felt the most important thing for the exorcism's success was the priest's disposition and those of his assistants. Few exorcists choose to work alone and usually he is assisted by at least three people. One of them is normally a junior priest who has been trained in exorcism procedures. He monitors the ritual and helps the exorcist, when possible, not to be distracted by the demon. Other assistants can be family members, seminary students or even medical doctors. The most important thing is that all of them be physically strong and as guiltless as possible. None of them can have any secret sins that the demon can use against them. As noted, a true possessed person will manifest the uncanny ability to tell of things that he or she cannot possibly know. In some cases, demons may shout out the sins of the exorcist or his assistants in an attempt to shame them or distract them and ruin the exorcism.

In his book, Martin also describes the setting where the exorcism takes place. It is usually a location where there is a connection between the demon and the victim, like the victim's bedroom or residence. This also provides a "comfort zone" for the victim so they will be more at ease and more willing to cooperate with the exorcism.

Although every exorcism is different, there are similar stages that they follow. In *Hostage to the Devil*, Martin describes the stages:

The Presence: The exorcist and his assistants become aware of the entity that is within the victim. The actions of the spirit appear to be the victim's actions but they are unlike the normal personality of the possessed. The exorcist's first job is to get past this demon's imitation of the victim and find out who the demon is, what it wants and how long it plans to stay. According to records, it is essential to try and learn the name of the demon. During the Middle Ages, a list was created of demonic entities that included more than 6,000 names.

Breakpoint: This is the moment when the demon's pretense of being the victim finally collapses and it can be a moment of confusion, panic and pandemonium. It is usually accompanied by a whirlwind of abuse, horrible sights, cursing, blasphemies, and loud noises, vomiting and overpowering odors. The demon then turns against the possessed and begins referring to him in the third person and as a victim.

The Voice: This is also regarded as a sign that the "Breakpoint" is at hand. The voice of the demon becomes "inordinately disturbing and humanly distressing babble." In order for the exorcism to proceed, the demon's voice must be silenced. This is another example of the evil spirit trying to interrupt or interfere with the exorcism.

The Clash: As the demon is silenced and the ritual prayers reach their highest point, both spiritual and physical pressures are applied against both the exorcist and the possessed. The exorcist is now in direct battle with the demon, urging the entity to reveal more information about itself so that it can be controlled.

Expulsion: As God's will triumphs over the situation, the demon leaves in the name of Jesus. Everyone who is present feels the presence dissipate and it often goes with fading voices and noises. In most cases, the victim will remember little, or perhaps even nothing, of the ordeal.

The solemn Great Exorcism Rite in the *Rituale Romanum* covers twenty-three printed pages. During the ritual, a number of items are usually present, including salt, which represents purity, and wine, representing the blood of Christ. The victim will be asked to hold a crucifix during the rite and the exorcist may also use holy water, religious medals, rosaries and relics, which may be physical items that were once a part of or objects touched or blessed by saints. The reading of the ritual begins with a series of prayers, psalm readings and an initial command for the unclean spirit, whoever he might be. Next, biblical passages concerning possession are read. The priest's stole and his right hand are placed on the possessed person and the specific words of exorcism are spoken. Interspersed by the sign of the cross, made on the possessed person's forehead and chest, the two exorcism passages are as follows:

I exorcise thee, most evil spirit, direct embodiment of our enemy, the entire entity and its whole legion, in the name of Jesus Christ, to go hence and escape from this creature of God. He, himself, commands thee, who is master from the heights of heaven to the depth of the earth. He who commands the sea, the winds and the tempests, now commands thee.

Listen, then, be filled with fear. O Satan, enemy of the Faith, enemy of the human race, who creates death and steals life, who destroys justice and is at the root of evil, who stimulates vice, tempts men, betrays nations, originated envy and greed, causes discord and brings suffering. Why dost thou remain and resist, when thou knowest that Christ the Lord will destroy thy strength? Fear him who was sacrificed in Isaac, sold in Joseph, and slaughtered in the Lamb, crucified in man, and yet is triumphant over Hell.

Depart, therefore, in the name of the Father and the Son and the Holy Ghost. Make way for the Holy Ghost, but the sign of the cross of Jesus Christ, our Lord, who with the Father and the Holy Ghost lives and reigns, one God, for ever and ever, world without end.

The second exorcism is as follows:

I adjure thee, thou old serpent, by the judge of the quick and the dead, by thy maker and the maker of the world, by him who has power to send thee to Hell, that thou depart quickly from this serpent of God ffiname of the possessed individualffl, who returns to the bosom of the Church, with fear and the affliction of thy terror. I adjure thee again, not in my own infirmity, but by the virtue of the Holy Ghost, that thou depart from this servant of God ffiname againffl, whom Almighty God hath made in his own image.

Yield, therefore; yield not to me but to the Ministry of Christ. For his power compels thee, he who subjugated thee to his cross. Tremble at his arms, he who led the souls to light after the lamentations of Hell had been subdued. May the body of man be a terror to thee, let the image of God be terrible to thee. Resist not, neither delay to flee this man ffiwomanffl, since it has pleased Christ to dwell in his ffiherffl body. And although thou knowest me to be a sinner, do not think me contemptible.

For it is God who commands thee.
The majesty of Christ commands thee.
God the father commands thee.
God the Son commands thee.
God the Holy Ghost commands thee.
The sacred cross commands thee.
The faith of the holy apostles Peter and Paul, and of all other saints, commands thee.

The exorcism cannot be expected to be achieved as the result of one rite, outlined in the *Rituale Romanum*, or without delays, frustrations and problems. When such a struggle occurs, the exorcist is advised to add a variety of prayers and readings from the Psalms. A "Prayer Following Liberation" may be said when complete success has been achieved. As mentioned earlier, the use of holy water, the laying on of hands and the placing of the priest's stole on the possessed person may also become part of the ceremony.

It can be a confusing and complicated series of events, all of which hopefully lead to success on the part of the exorcist. But is this success, when it does occur, really an expulsion of demonic spirits? Or could the successful exorcism be nothing more than a "spiritual placebo" that convinces the victim that whatever was plaguing them has departed? Many believe this to be the case and are often

22

torn between the danger of playing into the delusions of a mentally ill person and the idea that whatever helps them must be a good thing.

Can exorcisms be dangerous? The answer seems to be "yes," to both the victim and the exorcist. But how dangerous can the ritual be? No one seems prepared to answer that but one thing is certain, the ritual is more cautiously employed by the Catholic Church today than it was in the past. When reviewing the conditions for demonic possession, there are many who dismiss them as nothing more than epilepsy, hysteria, schizophrenia and other psychological disorders. For this reason, priests are cautioned to be as certain as possible that the person is truly demonically possessed before performing the ritual. In the Catholic Church, an exorcist must have the express permission of the archdiocese before beginning the ritual.

Exorcisms are not, and have not been for the past century or so, something that is entered into lightly. Careful preparations must be made and those attempting the exorcism must be sure that they are up to the task. A passage from the Bible illustrates what can happen to those who don't take exorcisms seriously. According to the story from the Book of Acts, several "itinerant Jewish exorcists" began trying to expel demons from the afflicted and their ritual included a phrase that cast out the demons "in the name of Jesus, whom Paul preaches, I command you to come out." During one such attempt, the evil spirit turned on the men and demanded of them "Jesus, I know, and I know about Paul, but who are you?" The possessed man then turned and attacked them like a wild animal. He beat the men mercilessly and stripped them of their clothing, throwing them into the street, naked and bleeding.

Is possession real? How much of the phenomena that is associated with exorcisms genuine and how much is imagination? What follows are some of the most famous - and perhaps even most authentic - cases of possession and exorcism in history. While I cannot vouch for the authenticity of each case, I can tell you that the events in these pages have been documented as the truth.

And if that doesn't have you turning on every light in the house while you're reading this, I don't know what will.

"PACT WITH SATAN"

At the age of sixteen, Clara Germana Cele told her confessor, Father Erasmus Horner, she had made a pact with Satan. This confession occurred at the Marianhill Order mission school in Umzinto, South Africa, where Clara had been living since the age of four. In the weeks that followed the girl's chilling words, Clara began to behave wildly and on August 20, 1906, she terrified the nuns in charge of the school by tearing off her clothes, breaking one of the posts on her bed, growling and grunting like an animal and appearing to converse with invisible beings. In more lucid moments, she begged the sisters to call for Father Horner. If they didn't, she said, Satan was going to kill her.

Before her strange confession, and the outbursts that followed, Clara had been considered a normal, healthy, although somewhat erratic young woman. As her condition worsened, she began to manifest signs of what the Church considered a case of authentic demonic possession. Holy water burned her when she was sprinkled with it but when she was sprinkled with ordinary water from the tap, she simply laughed. She complained loudly whenever a crucifix was brought into her presence and she could detect a religious object, like a rosary or medal, even when it was heavily wrapped or otherwise concealed.

One of the outstanding features of the possession was the great physical strength that the girl manifested whenever she was under demonic control. She battered those who tried to control her and in the early days of the possession, she brutally attacked two nuns who accused her of faking her condition. The two nuns were accompanied by three large assistants when they came to watch over Clara one evening. At first, Clara was quiet and subdued but soon, she began to ask "tricky questions," apparently of a theological nature, of the sisters and an argument began. Father Horner later wrote that before anyone could realize what was going on, Clara "stood before the sisters in blazing anger and upbraided them in a manner that would always remember for its lack of devotion and grace."

When the nuns tried to strike the girl, Clara ran for the door, locked it and put the key into her pocket. Then she grabbed the two nuns by their habits, shook them and, with incredible strength, slammed one into a corner and threw the other to the far side of the room. Clara severely beat one of the sisters, tore the veil from her head and then pushed her under the bed. With great speed, she jumped on top of the other nun, who was crouching in the corner in fear, and choked and beat her as well. The three assistants cowered in terror during the assault, too frightened to come near the girl.

Mysterious fires also sprang up in Clara's presence. Once, when she entered a kitchen where a small coal fire was burning, a huge flame suddenly shot into the air. While others who were present screamed and ran away, Clara only laughed and seemed to bask in the heat. The room then seemed to fill with flames, even though only a few half-glowing pieces of coal had remained in the kitchen ashes. On another occasion, another fire broke out as the girls were going to bed and when Clara was surrounded by twenty other girls on both sides of her. The girls had just entered their dormitory and the room supervisor, Sister Juliana, was resting in a nearby chair. A few moments after Clara climbed into bed, the

24

bed frame started to make a loud creaking sound and then flames rushed out from underneath it. They subsided when Sister Juliana sprinkled holy water on the bed. When the bed was later examined, the bed and bed posts were found to be charred but the girl's bed clothes and blankets were completely untouched.

Strange sounds and explained noises were also frequently heard around Clara. Often during the night, loud noises could be heard at the door of the dormitory where the girls slept. Father Horner and another priest armed themselves and began to guard the house, thinking that an outsider who was hostile to the mission school might be at work, trying to frighten the young women and the nuns. The two priests occupied an empty room close to the women's sleeping quarters and as they began their vigil, found everything to be quiet. Things did not stay quiet for long. Father Horner wrote:

Suddenly, at ten o'clock, there was a sound like a thunderclap at the door. Inside, everyone cried out in fear and horror. We hurried outside to find out what was going on. Then, once again, one, two, five tremendous blows. We went out once more, and again there was nothing in sight. Banging and pounding could be heard on several doors inside the house. We went to investigate and found nothing. The noise and pounding continued in the rooms of the brothers, in the smithy, in the storage section, and even in the shed where the animals had become restless, but nowhere was there anything to be seen. The noise stopped by eleven-fifteen.

The events did not end with insistent pounding on the doors. The sounds of horse's hooves were also frequently heard. Those at the mission often heard the sounds of rapidly approaching horses, as though a band of riders was nearly at the school. Needless to say, these sounds wreaked havoc on those present. "Everyone yelled," Father Horner wrote, "and people ran in all directions, but when we looked back, there was nothing to be seen." On another occasion, he stated, "the heavy sound of passing horses could be heard overtaking us, but again nothing was to be seen." He also reported that a sound was heard that "suggested something falling off the roof, but there was no visible cause." Seemingly exhausted by all of this, Horner concludes this section of his report with a simple phrase: "Well, there was a good deal of this sort of thing."

The idea that Clara was engaged in some sort of hoax began to fade as the strange events continued, particularly when everyone saw how much she suffered during the times when she was allegedly under demonic control. Father Horner repeatedly reported to his superiors about the incredible speed with which Clara moved when she was visibly possessed. Another curious capacity that astonished the priests and nuns was her ability to transform into a snake-like

25

creature. Her whole body seemed to become as flexible as rubber and she would writhe and slither, her neck seeming to elongate like a serpent. Father Horner wrote that she "sometimes moved on her back, at other times on her belly, with snake-like motions" and "when she moved backwards, her head settled on the ground as if it were a foot and her whole body moved downward, snake fashion." On one occasion, while a nun was kneeling before her in prayer, Clara darted at her in "typical snake manner" and bit the woman on her arm. Where the girl's teeth had left their mark, a reddish point showed at the center and a small wound resembling a snake bite appeared.

In addition to being credited with the ability to run up a wall, two yards high, with such speed that "it seemed she was moving on solid ground", Clara was also said to be able to defy gravity while under demonic control. Although rarely seen outside of the realm of stage magicians and questionable accounts of spirit mediums, Clara was said to levitate during times of possession. Father Horner wrote:

She floated often three, four and up to five feet in the air, sometimes vertically, with her feet downward, and at other times horizontally, with her whole body floating above her bed. She was in a rigid position. Even her clothing did not fall downward, as would have been normal; instead, her dresses remained tightly attached to her body and legs. If she was sprinkled with holy water, she moved down immediately, and her clothing fell loosely onto her bed. This type of phenomenon took place in the presence of witnesses, including outsiders. Even in church, where she could be seen by everyone, she floated above her seat. Some people tried to pull her down forcibly, holding on to her feet, but it proved to be impossible.

Father Horner's account should not leave the impression that Clara was in a state of relaxation as she levitated above her bed. On the contrary, levitation occurred during periods of such physical and verbal violence that she often had to be restrained and tied up to keep her from destroying property or hurting those who were nearby. He wrote about one of these incidents:

Everyone sought to help, but it still took another three hours before we were finally able to get handcuffs on the girl as she was in a state of violent anger. Both her arms were stiff and immovable. At the same time, and amid horrible noise and disturbance, she was, over and over again, levitated off the ground while sitting in her chair.

Permission to perform an exorcism on Clara, to rid her of diabolical possession, was issued by the local Bishop on September 10, 1906, slightly less than a month before the incidents began. Father Erasmus Horner was assisted in the rite by the house father of the mission, Father Mansuet. As was standard during exorcisms, the diabolical entity believed to be inside of the girl was asked to identify itself. Using a voice much different from that of Clara, it identified itself and gave several names, such as "Yiminia" and either "Balek" or "Malek." When pressed for accuracy, the voice replied, "We do not all have names. Only the important ones have names, not those that are small and insignificant. I am small and insignificant."

The rites of exorcism began the following morning, ended at noon and then began again at 3:00 p.m. that afternoon. The rituals lasted late into the night and then started once more the following morning. As with the days leading up to the exorcism, Clara had moments of clarity and peace during the process. Alternating between states of diabolical possession and her normal personality, she was able to take part in confession and communion. This however, involved great spiritual risks, of which Father Horner quickly became aware. She often asked him to hear her confession, just to have a few moments of respite from the possession. He said that hearing her confession was a difficult task because he could not be sure if it was Clara or the demon who spoke to him. In some cases, a self-dialogue seemed to be going on -- as if two beings were speaking through Clara's mouth.

Father Horner also noted that he had to very careful during Holy Communion, as "Satan tempted her constantly." Clara seemed to be tempted to spit out the communion wine or to withdraw the wafer from her mouth and degrade it in some manner. At other times, she was unable to swallow at all. She gagged and strained but the back of her mouth remained rigid. When Father Horner placed two fingers on her neck, though, this difficulty disappeared instantly. She often trembled and shook during the communion, spilling the wine, even when she had assistance. In many cases, though, she quieted down and listened to prayer and on these evenings, after a peaceful communion, the service was followed by the times of the most vicious attacks. As Father Horner wrote, "Those were the times of Satan's revenge."

In addition to the spiritual risks of Clara's exorcism, there were the physical risks to the girl --- and to the exorcists too. While in the midst of a severe possession crisis, while Clara was raving and acting destructively, Father Mansuet began the exorcism ritual. With his stole draped around his neck and across his shoulders, he began reading from the *Rituale Romanum*. He was soon interrupted by a voice speaking through Clara. When the priest commanded the voice to be silent, Clara began to react violently, straining at the bonds that held her to her bed. The voice raged at him and momentarily losing control, the priest slapped the girl across the face. Instantly speaking in Clara's voice again, the young woman cried and asked why he was beating her -- unaware of what she had been doing and saying just moments before.

Regretful, the priest leaned down to comfort the girl and as he did so, the demon returned. Snapping out of her restraints, Clara knocked the prayer book from his hands and in a quick movement, tore the stole from his neck and ripped it to shreds. As Father Mansuet tried to scramble away, Clara seized hold of him by the neck, choking him and throwing him to the ground. The priest tried to fight back but was no match for Clara's brutal strength. She hammered him against the bed post and then shoved him under the bed. Moments later, the demonic rage vanished and Clara began to weep. She cowered into the corner as the priest gingerly crawled out from beneath the bed. His fingers were badly bruised and his body was covered with scratches and abrasions. When Clara saw what she had apparently done, she began to weep. She was still sitting in the corner, apparently shattered with grief, when others came into the room to see what the commotion was about.

The exorcism rites continued with several hopeful days and a number of setbacks, like the one that occurred after Father Horner announced that he had to make a trip to Europe. Clara asked him not to go, or at least to postpone the trip, but he was unable to do so. While he was away, the girl experienced a relapse, announcing that she had made a new pact with the Devil. Horner was stunned and heartsick by this latest development but encouraged by the fact that Clara wanted the exorcism to continue.

In April 1907, the rituals began again and were only interrupted by a visit from the Apostolic Vicar, Dr. Henri Delalle, Bishop of Natal, who came to the mission to see if Clara's possession was indeed genuine. Accompanied by others, Bishop Delalle checked the girl's condition and verified that she was authentically possessed. The new exorcism began on April 24.

Although Father Horner and the others continued to be discouraged by some of the problems they faced, Clara herself insisted that the exorcism be continued. It lasted for two more days and then, at last, the demon departed, leaving behind a stench that "could not be compared with anything else."

The horrible events were now over and Clara began a normal life, unhampered by the threat of possession. She stayed on at the mission for the next seven years, living an ordinary and peaceful life. Sadly, though, she died on March 14, 1912 during a tuberculosis outbreak. She was only twenty-three-years-old.

EXORCISM IN IOWA

Although the St. Louis Exorcism of 1949 has become one of the best-known examples of alleged demonic possession in recent history, there was actually another, much less publicized case that occurred two decades before in Earling, Iowa. This case is perhaps just as puzzling and just as dramatic as the St. Louis case but is much more obscure, likely because it never inspired a book and a movie to be made about it. The case of Emma Schmidt has become known as one of the most chilling and horrific cases of possession in American history and is one that was well-documented by those who were present. The exorcism lasted for an incredible twenty-three days and no one involved ever stopped having nightmares about the terrible events that occurred.

The events actually began a number of years before their culmination in Iowa. At that time, Emma was a young woman in Wisconsin. She led an ordinary life until the death of her father. After that event, she began to act in a strange manner that became a mystery to her friends and neighbors. In later years, Emma would say that her father had cursed her upon his death because she had refused to give in to the incestuous demands that he placed on her after her mother had died. Emma always believed that her father had handed her over to the Devil.

Whatever the reason, Emma began to behave strangely after her father died. The once sensitive and religious young woman became increasingly angry,

29

hurling obscenities and laughing inappropriately during church services and in public places. Many of the local people who had known the girl her entire life remarked on the bizarre changes in her personality. Doctors who examined her first believed that she was either hysterical or prone to nervous spells and hallucinations but could find absolutely nothing wrong with her. She was a medical mystery, they thought, and ran test after test. All of them proved to be negative -- but there was obviously something wrong.

After exhausting the doctors, Emma appealed to the church for help. Several of the priests that she spoke with agreed with the findings of the physicians, that Emma was clearly hysterical and in need of psychiatric help. Others disagreed -- the woman understood languages that she had neither heard nor read, they claimed. When a priest blessed her in Latin, she foamed at the mouth with rage. If she handled an object that was sprinkled with holy water, she would scream curses and blasphemies and throw it against the wall. Slowly, very slowly, it began to be realized that there was something going on with this woman that could not easily be dismissed. The Church had always taken the rite of exorcism seriously and only after intense study and observation, and the passing of a number of years, did the priests agree that Emma was actually possessed by one or more evil spirits.

Father Theophilus Riesinger, a Capuchin monk and a man with past experience with exorcisms, agreed to take on the case. He knew Emma well, as she was a member of his parish in Marathon, Wisconsin, but he wanted to protect her privacy as much as possible. He made arrangements for her to travel to Earling, Iowa and for the ritual to take place at the convent of the Franciscan Sisters in that small town. Joseph Steiger, the parish priest at Earling, was a long-time friend of Father Theophilus, but he was not eager for the exorcism to take place in his parish. It was only after urging from his friend and the Mother Superior of the convent that he agreed.

Emma traveled to Earling by train, passing the time alone and filled with desperate worry over what was about to take place. She knew that she wanted the demons to be banished from her but she was also overwhelmed with anger and rage, apparently brought on by the evil spirits that plagued her. When she stepped off the train at the station, she waved her arms wildly at the nuns who came to collect her. She screamed at them and called them foul names before inexplicably going limp. The startled -- but dedicated - sisters gathered Emma and her belongings and helped her into their car. The group rode in silence to the convent.

Father Theophilus arrived later that evening but the first signs of trouble had already begun with Emma. A well-meaning nun in the kitchen had sprinkled her food with holy water and the enraged Emma threw it on the floor, screaming that the food smelled horrible. When unblessed food was substituted for the first tray, she devoured it, almost without chewing. There was no way that Emma could have known that either tray, containing the same items -- except for the holy water -- was different from the other.

The exorcism began early the next morning. Emma was brought into a room that had been set aside for the ritual and placed on the mattress of an iron bed. The sleeves and the skirt of her dress were tightly bound and Father Theophilus instructed several of the nuns to hold her firmly to the bed. The exorcist, with Father Steiger standing beside him, began to pray. Then, as she would on every day that followed, Emma sank into unconsciousness. Her eyes closed so tightly that they could not be forced open.

Almost as soon as she entered the trance state, however, she tore loose from the sisters who were holding her and by some mysterious energy, reportedly flung her body from the bed, into the air, and against a nearby wall. She was pinned there by a force so strong that neither priest could pull her free. The nuns, now trembling with fright, tugged at her until they finally were able to pull her loose and returned her to the bed. Moments later, the exorcism continued and Emma began to howl -- although according to the statements of those present, her mouth never opened. Howling, inhuman sounds and guttural growls issued forth from her throat, but her lips never moved.

News of the exorcism spread through the nearby community and people came from all over the surrounding area to see for themselves what was happening at the convent. Crowds assembled beneath the windows of the room where Emma was kept but many of them left, reportedly unable to stand the excruciating sounds that issued from inside.

Over the course of the next few days, those inside the room endured the ordeal with Emma. The twelve nuns took turns attending to her, afterwards leaving the building to get fresh air, and often to weep. Only Father Theophilus remained composed. Emma, seemingly helpless to what was happening to her, continually frothed at the mouth and then spewed out torrents of stinking vomit that filled both pitchers and pails. She had scarcely eaten for days and yet was said to have thrown up as many as thirty times in one day. On several occasions, when the exorcist brought the Blessed Sacrament near Emma, he saw her flesh twist and contort, as though something was moving beneath her skin.

The exorcism continued from early in the morning until late at night, every day, hour after hour. The bellowing voices and cries continued to come from the stricken woman and the howling, like that of an animal, broke the usual stillness of the convent. At times, the voices became so frightening that Father Steiger and the nuns fled from the room. Father Theophilis persisted in his task, though, praying and calling for the devils to leave Emma. His work was so strenuous

31

that he often had to change his sweat-soaked clothing as many as three times a day.

During the sessions, a number of voices allegedly came through Emma. They claimed to be various demons and evil spirits from her past, including her father, who had tried to force her to have sex with him, and even her father's mistress, who according to the priest's report, had murdered her own children. During this manifestation, Emma was said to have vomited with such violence that Father Theophilus and Father Steiger had to use towels to clean the fluid from their clothing.

Whatever was expressing itself in these voices, it demonstrated an uncanny knowledge of things that could not have been known to Emma. On one occasion, as a test, a piece of paper with a Latin inscription was placed on Emma's head. The nuns, thinking the words were a prayer, were surprised to see that the demons tolerated its presence. The words actually had no religious content at all. However, when a second piece of paper, which had been secretly blessed, was placed on Emma's head, it was immediately ripped to pieces.

As the exorcism continued, day after day, Emma was unable to eat and the nuns were only able to get liquid down her throat. In a short time, it would usually come right back up again. Her now emaciated body was said to no longer resemble anything human. Her head swelled and her features distorted. Her eyes bulged and her lips bloated to twice their normal size. Her face was flushed with heat as her skin stretched and took on an unnatural shine. They were so swollen that the nuns feared that her skin might actually burst. In spite of the fact that she could not eat and she lost a tremendous amount of weight, those who attended to Emma claimed that her body became so inexplicably heavy that the iron bed on which she rested bent and curved so that it almost touched the floor.

As the exhausting days passed, a change came over Father Steiger. He developed a strong dislike for the entire procedure -- almost a hatred -- and began to dislike Father Theophilus, his old friend. In one bout of anger, he screamed at the exorcist and called him foul names, but Father Theophilis took it in stride, explaining that the demons were using the priest against him as a weapon. The more he tried to save Emma, the worse the abuse became. As the voices that came from Emma began berating Father Steiger, his friend commanded that they leave him alone. The battle was with him, he shouted. But the voices only laughed and continued to threaten Father Steiger. "Just wait until Friday..." they warned.

Sick of the constant howling, Father Steiger learned to ignore the voices but then on Friday, a day he had been warned about, he nearly lost his life. It happened as he was returning from performing the last rites for the mother of a local farmer. On his return to Earling, he crossed a bridge over a ravine and would later claim that a large, black cloud suddenly descended on the car. Unable to see, he yanked the vehicle into low gear but it was too late to stop. The automobile veered to the side and collided with the steel railings of the bridge. Metal smashed and glass shattered and the car tore through the rails until it was left hanging, teetering on the edge of the ravine. A farmer who was plowing a field a short distance away heard the crash and came running. He managed to pull Father Steiger from the wreckage. The priest was stunned and numb with shock, but unhurt.

The farmer was kind enough to drive him to the convent and when he arrived, he went straight to Emma's room. As he walked in, she began laughing uproariously. A guttural voice from inside of her laughed at the priest and celebrated the destruction of his car. Father Theophilus and the nuns were shocked and asked if this was true. Father Steiger agreed that it was but added that the demon did not have the strength to hurt him personally. The voice cursed and stated that only the priest's patron saint had saved his life.

On several occasions after this, Father Steiger continued to be bedeviled by the spirits. He was often awakened at night by knocking coming from inside of his walls, scratching noises and weird banging sounds that would often last throughout the night.

But none of this could match the suffering endured by Emma Schmidt. She continued to lose consciousness each day as the exorcism began and would only awaken late at night when it was over. She remembered nothing of what transpired during the day, the violent sickness that she suffered from or the horrible curses that came from her mouth. Increasingly frailer from this daily ordeal, she was soon no longer able to walk. She had to be carried back and forth between her private quarters and the exorcism room. The nuns feared that she might die before the exorcism could end.

The records say that the events continued for more than two weeks before there was any indication that the spirits might be forced out of Emma's body. At that point, Father Theophilus doubled his efforts and for three days and nights, he continued the exorcism without sleep and with very little rest. In addition to what must have been nerves of steel, the priest also seemed to have incredible powers of endurance. But even so, toward the end of the third night, he became so weak that he nearly collapsed. He prayed to God to spare his life and finally, the marathon session was finished.

The end seemed to be near and later, the nuns would testify that a miraculous figure appeared to Emma one day and urged her not to give up hope. The nuns claimed that they saw a cluster of white roses appear on the ceiling of the room but it disappeared before Father Steiger could be brought in. Regardless, the sign gave hope to the priest and he and Father Theophilus both knew that the horror was finally reaching its climax.

More days of pain and exhaustion followed but on September 23, 1928, at 9:00 p.m., Emma Schmidt jerked free from the hands of the nuns who held her and she stood up on the bed with only her heels still touching the mattress. Fearful that she might be hurled against the wall again -- or perhaps this time the ceiling -- Father Steiger urged the sisters to pull her back down. As they reached for her, Father Theophilus blessed her and demanded once more that the demons depart from her. At that moment, Emma reportedly collapsed and the sounds of screams and piercing voices filled the room.

Everyone present froze as Emma contorted one last time and then opened her eyes and smiled. As she looked from one fact to another, she began to weep. Her torment was over -- the exorcism was finished at last. Everyone was so happy that it took them several seconds to notice the stomach-churning smell of human waste that filled the room. It was the final indignity left behind by the departing spirits, it was said. The nuns opened all of the windows and a fresh cool breeze blew across the sills, driving out the foul odors.

There was little to say in the aftermath of the Earling case. Had Emma Schmidt truly been plagued by demons or evil spirits? The exorcism caused a heated debate among members of the Catholic Church, as many of them continued to believe that she was a troubled woman who had been in the grips of hysteria. This may have been the case, but even if it was, Emma lived a quiet and peaceful life after the exorcism was over and was never bothered by her troubles again. For the rest of his life, Father Theophilus maintained that she had been possessed and Father Steiger and the Franciscan sisters agreed.

Some have wondered if perhaps the events that occurred in Iowa may have somehow influenced details in exorcisms that were still to be reported in the years to come. Could the alleged victims, like the boy in the St. Louis Exorcism case, have read of this earlier case and simply mimicked what was reported? In those days, aside from biblical accounts, there were no details available so that someone could "fake" being possessed well enough to fool a priest. There were no films to see and very few books written on the subject to make the material readily available. The 1928 Iowa exorcism was no exception either. The first account of it appeared in a 1935 booklet called "Begone Satan!" and it was written in German by a priest named Vogl, who interviewed the participants first-hand. The booklet was later translated and published by the Reverend Celestine Kapsner of St. John's Abbey in Collegeville, Minnesota. Only a few hundred of them were ever printed and the story was soon forgotten. It would not surface again until the middle 1970s, after *The Exorcist* became popular. The limited availability of the story seems to rule out any influence that it might have had on later cases -- but few would be able to dismiss the similarities that were present in cases that would emerge in years to come.

"THE EXORCISM OF EMILY ROSE" CASE

Aside from *The Exorcist*, there are few movies about possession that have chilled audiences in the way that the 2005 film, *The Exorcism of Emily Rose*, has been able to do. What many are unaware of, though, is that the film was based on an actual case that occurred in Germany in the middle 1970s. It was a terrifying story of both exorcism and death and not only did the victim in the case not survive but two priests involved in the case were convicted of her murder.

Anneliese Michel was born on September 21, 1952 and was raised in a normal, happy family in the town of Klingenberg am Main, Bavaria. Her father, Josef, operated a profitable sawmill in town and he and Anneliese's mother, Anna, were strict Catholics, who raised their daughter to be religiously devout. Her life changed one day in 1968 when she began shaking and found that she was unable to control her body. Her seizures were so extreme that she was unable to call out for her parents or her three sisters. They were terrified when they discovered her, having collapsed on the floor, and she was rushed to the hospital. A neurologist at the Psychiatric Clinic in Würzburg diagnosed her with epilepsy. Because of the seriousness of the seizures, and the severity of the depression that followed, Anneliese was admitted for treatment at the hospital.

Even though she was still suffering from seizures, and unknown to anyone was also experiencing visions of demonic faces during her daily prayers, Anneliese was able to return to school in the fall of 1970 and went on to the University of Würzburg in September 1973, where she began studying elementary education.

Anneliese was still experiencing the horrific visions that had started to plague her in the hospital and by now, she was hearing voices too. She finally confessed to her doctors and her parents that the voices were starting to give her orders and threatening that they would take her to hell. The doctors were unable to help her and the medicine that she was given did not seem to chase away the eerie sights and sounds. Finally, possibly because of her strict Catholic background, Anneliese became convinced that she was possessed. After four years of medical treatment, her condition and her depression continued to worsen and soon her parents began to share her fears of demonic intervention in her life.

In the summer of 1973, her parents visited several different pastors, pleading for an exorcism for their daughter. Their requests were denied and they were given recommendations to have Anneliese continue with her treatment and medication. It was explained to them that the process by which the Church proves a possession is strictly defined and until all of the criteria is met including aversion to religious objects, speaking in a foreign language that the victims does not know, paranormal powers and more a bishop cannot approve an exorcism. Anneliese continued to suffer from her illness -- as well as the visions and voices -- as she began her college studies.

In 1974, it seemed that Anneliese might finally be receiving some assistance from the Church. After supervising the young woman for some time, Pastor Ernst Alt, a local parish priest and a specialist in exorcism, requested permission to perform an exorcism from the Bishop of Würzburg, Josef Stangl. The request was denied and the Bishop suggested that Anneliese try and live a more religious lifestyle in order to find peace.

A change in her already stringent religious lifestyle offered no relief. The attacks did not diminish and Anneliese's behavior started to become more erratic. At her parent's house in Klingenberg, she wreaked havoc on everything -- and everyone -- she came into contact with. She insulted, berated and screamed at her family. She constantly assaulted them, hitting and beating her parents and her sisters and biting them with savage force. She refused to eat because the "demons would not allow it." She slept on the stone floor in the basement, ate spiders, flies, and pieces of coal and even began drinking her own urine. She could be heard screaming throughout the house for hours and ran about breaking crucifixes, destroying religious paintings and tearing apart rosaries. Anneliese also began mutilating herself, cutting her arms and legs to see the cuts bleed, tearing off her clothes and raising her skirts to squat and urinate on the floor without warning.

Although no details are available as to how it happened, Bishop Stangl was eventually worn down about his decision to allow an exorcism for Anneliese. He had consulted with a leading expert on demonic possession, Father Adolf Rodewyk, who agreed with Father Alt about Anneliese's condition. Father Rodewyk recommended that the exorcism proceed and in September 1975, Bishop Stangl verified the conditions of possession and assigned Father Arnold Renz and Father Ernst Alt to perform the ritual. For the next eleven months, all medical treatment of Anneliese was stopped and the rites of exorcism were carried out secretly in the bedroom of her parent's home during one-hour sessions. The attacks that she suffered from during the exorcism were sometimes so strong that she had to be held down by three men or even chained to the floor. During this time, Anneliese found that her life outside of the

36

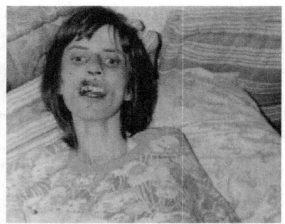

Anneliese Michel during her school years and right at the height of the
exorcism - and shortly before her death.

exorcism rituals had returned to a semblance of normalcy. She was able to go to
church and return to school for a time, taking final examinations at the
Pedagogic Academy in Würzburg.

As time passed, though, Anneliese either became sicker or continued to be
possessed - depending on what you believe. Her symptoms began to return, not
just during the exorcism sessions, and she would often find herself paralyzed or
passing out. The exorcism went on, stretching over the weeks and months,
always with the same prayers and readings from the *Rituale Romanum.*
Anneliese refused to eat for days at a time and eventually, her knees ruptured
from the six hundred genuflections a respectful bowing on one knee while
making the sign of a cross, which is usually done when entering a church that
she performed obsessively throughout the exorcism. Anneliese's parents, and the
priests involved, made over forty audio tapes of the rituals, in order to preserve
the details.

The last exorcism session was held on June 30, 1976. By this time, Anneliese
had contracted pneumonia, was totally emaciated and running a high fever. She
was too exhausted to physically perform the genuflections of the ceremony but
her parents held her up and walked her through the motions. "Beg for
absolution," was the last statement that Anneliese made to the priests. To her
mother, she said "Mama, I'm afraid." She died that night at the age of twenty-
three from starvation. The autopsy report, which recorded her weight at only
sixty-eight pounds, stated that her death was caused by malnutrition and
dehydration that resulted from almost a year of semi-starvation during the
exorcism.

37

Anna Michel reported the death of her daughter on July 1. Later that same day, Pastor Alt gave details of the events to the authorities in Aschaffenburg. Officials began an immediate investigation but prosecutors took more than two years to file charges and bring the case to the courts. Anneliese's parents and the two exorcists, Father Alt and Father Renz, were accused of negligent homicide for refusing to bring a medical doctor into the case. According to the evidence, Anneliese had "starved to death." Specialists claimed that if she had been force fed even a week before her death, her life could have been saved.

The trial started on March 30, 1978. A series of doctors that testified all basically told the court that Anneliese had died from a combination of epilepsy, mental disorders and an extreme religious environment that, in the words of Professor Hans Sattes of the University of Wurzburg, added up to "a spiritual sickness and heavy psychic disturbance."

Throughout the trial, Josef Michel sat impassively, listening to the testimony through a special amplifier that allowed him to hear. His wife, Anna, steadily took notes, pausing only to moan "Oh, dear God," whenever a doctor alleged that that her daughter was not possessed but had a mental disorder. Father Renz stayed quiet during the trial, but presented an imposing figure in his priest's robes, with his long gray hair swept straight back and no emotion on his face. Father Alt, who wore civilian clothing during the proceedings, was the one most involved in the trial and he offered advice to the attorneys that allowed nothing to pass that could be challenged.

The two priests were defended by lawyers paid for by the Church. Anneliese's parents were defended by one of Germany's top attorneys, Erich Schmidt-Leichner, who had made a name for himself during the Nazi war crimes trials following World War II. He claimed that not only was exorcism legal but that the German constitution protected citizens in the unrestricted exercise of their religious beliefs.

The prosecution offered a number of psychiatrists as expert witnesses and they spoke about "Doctrinaire Induction," claiming the priests gave Anneliese the contents of her psychotic behavior. They also blamed the film *The Exorcist* as an influence on her beliefs. Consequently, they said, she later accepted her behavior as a form of demonic possession. They also agreed that Anneliese's unsettled sexual development, along with her diagnosed Temporal Lobe Epilepsy, had influenced the psychosis.

The defense countered their arguments with evidence they believed showed the girl had actually been possessed. The evidence, in addition to witness statements, included the audio tapes that were made during the exorcism sessions. The tapes were filled with the sounds of the young woman's screams and howls, as well as the exorcist's prayers and a number of strange voices that came from Anneliese and yet were clearly not her regular pattern of speech. In some segments, different voices argued with one another and the exorcists claimed that the voices were demons inside of Anneliese, fighting over which of them would have to leave her body first. No one involved with the exorcism had any doubt that Anneliese was genuinely possessed. Father Renz and Father Alt were convinced that she had been possessed and that it had only been her death that freed her from her demons. She was now, they believed, with God.

In the end, the accused were found guilty of manslaughter resulting from negligence and were given a six-month suspended sentence. The jury had no choice but to find them guilty based on the evidence that was presented but were so unsettled by the audio tapes that were played, along with the conviction of the exorcists, that a light sentence was handed down. The prosecutor dismissed this idea, however, and stated that he felt that the parents should not be punished because they had suffered enough.

Regardless of the reasons behind the verdict, the case was finally over. The trial, called the Klingenberg Case, became the basis for the 2005 film *The Exorcism of Emily Rose*. The film slightly deviated from the real events for example, it is set in the United States and Anneliese was re-named Emily Rose but it presented the most chilling aspects of the story and like the real-life case allowed viewers to decide for themselves whether or not the main character was actually possessed or not.

This remains the biggest question to arise from the Anneliese Michel case. Was the young woman really possessed? Those who were directly involved in the case maintain that she was, citing her visions and the voices that she heard, her aversion to religious objects and the terrifying recordings as evidence. But did the case really fit the criteria set forth by the Catholic Church? And if not, why was the exorcism suggested by an expert in possession, Father Rodewyk, and then sanctioned by Bishop Stangl?

For the Church, the death of Anneliese was a nightmare come true, demonstrating the dangers of involved in exorcisms and the murky responsibilities of the priest when it comes to spiritual and medical care. Father Rodewyk himself wrote a handbook on exorcisms in 1963 and in it, he urged priests to consider medical explanations for apparent possessions. He also outlined the bishop's responsibilities saying that he "may appoint a commission of theologians and physicians to undertake a further investigation" and warns that exorcists "must guard against playing the role of physician when encountering psychological symptoms."

These were mere warnings, though, for the *Rituale Romanum* did not state that a doctor must be in attendance during the exorcism. This deficiency in church procedure was corrected, in Germany at least, after the conviction of the two priests in the Michel case. In May 1978, the German Bishop's Conference ruled that in the future no exorcisms would be permitted unless a doctor was present.

While this may have protected future victims of possession, and those who might possibly be possessed, it did nothing for Anneliese Michel. Her death had been a tragedy -- no matter what the cause -- and remains a mystery to this day. Was she a delusional young woman who, in the belief that she was possessed, starved herself to death? Were her parents and her priests, the people she trusted the most in the world, ultimately responsible for her demise?

Or was she, as those same people believed, truly possessed by demonic spirits? Did these demons break down her defenses to the point that only death could free her from their clutches?

The story of Anneliese Michel remains as mysterious as any within the annals of possession and exorcism. What really happened? Those of us who can only read about the case, looking backward on history, will never really know for sure. Only those who were actually present can know what was heard, seen and experienced and to make matters worse, we cannot even be sure that their perceptions can be trusted. Were their minds clouded by fear, by religion or perhaps, simplest of all, by the confusing and convoluted nature of what was occurring?

As the reader has become aware during the preceding pages, demonic, or spirit, possession can be bizarre, terrifying and unearthly -- and in many cases, can stretch the limits of credibility. How do we know that any of the reports of "demonic forces" actually occurred? How do we know these stories are nothing more than creative imaginations at work? To put it simply -- we don't.

It is not my purpose to debunk the idea of demonic possession or to try and convince the reader of the reality of it either. In the pages that follow, we'll take a look at one of the most compelling cases of possession in American history and we'll take a look at it from every side. Can I tell you that every aspect of the story is true? Of course not, but I will present the evidence for you to examine and then you can judge the truth - or lies - of the story for yourself.

PART ONE:

MARYLAND'S "HAUNTED BOY"

The mother, grandmother and boy while lying on the bed on this night heard something coming toward them similar to the rhythm of marching feet and the beat of drums. The sound would travel the length of the mattress and then back again, and repeat this action until the mother asked: "Is this you, Aunt Tillie?"

From The "Exorcist's Diary", a case study kept by the Jesuits in the 1949 case

The "St. Louis Exorcism Case" began not in St. Louis but in one of two Washington D.C. suburbs, the small Maryland towns of Cottage City or Mount Rainier. There exists some debate over this because there have been a couple of different houses that have been identified as the home that belonged to the family of the possessed boy. As most readers already know, what has come to be known as the "St. Louis Exorcism Case" would go on to inspire William Peter Blatty's 1971 best-selling book and the movie based on it, *The Exorcist.* In the novel, a young girl is possessed by a demon and is subjected to an exorcism by Catholic priests. In the true story, though, the subject of the alleged possession was not a girl but a boy who has been identified in various accounts as "Roland" or "Robbie Doe." Robbie as we will call him here was born in 1935 and grew up in this area. He was the only child of a dysfunctional family and had a troubled childhood.

41

Author's note: Yes, I do know the real name of "Robbie Doe" and even interviewed him during the research for the original edition of this book. It's easy to find, based on property records for some of the locations mentioned in the story. However, when I did the first interview with him in the late 1990s, his name was not common knowledge and I agreed that I would not use it in any of my writings. So, regardless of the fact that a number of tactless people have posted Robbie's name on the internet, in this book, I will continue to refer to his as "Robbie Doe."

The debate about the location of the house came about a few years ago when it was written that the house was located 3807 40th Avenue in Cottage City. Others disagreed and said that the house was actually located at 3210 Bunker Hill Road in Mount Rainer. As it turns out, both arguments may be correct because the family later moved from Cottage City to Mount Rainer and also because it has been shown that the house on 40th Avenue was actually occupied by another family in 1950. This means that the family had moved out prior to this, apparently to Mount Rainer. A correspondent of mine, who provided much of the information that I have about the house and the family who lived there, grew up in Mount Rainer and lived a short distance away from 3210 Bunker Hill Road. It was not hard to discover the name of the boy and his family once this information was obtained. My contact stated that "the house at the corner of Bunker Hill Road and 33rd street was burned down in 1966. I should know, because I was born in Mount Rainier, Maryland and I lived at 4100 33rd street until I was nine. The house at 3210 Bunker Hill Road was exactly five houses away from mine. I remember it well as I was terrified to walk by it. Not because I knew the history no one knew then but because it was quite scary-looking and it sat about thirty yards from the front steps."

In January 1949, the family of thirteen-year-old "Robbie Doe" began to be disturbed by scratching sounds that came from inside of the walls and ceilings of the house. Believing that the house was infested with mice, the parents called an exterminator but he could find no sign of rodents. To make matters worse, his efforts seemed to add to the problem. Noises that sounded like someone walking in the hallway could be heard and dishes and objects were often found to be moved without explanation.

And while the noises were disturbing, they weren't nearly as frightening as when Robbie began to be attacked. His bed shook so hard that he couldn't sleep at night. His blankets and sheets were torn from the bed. When he tried to hold onto them, he was reportedly pulled off the bed and onto the floor with the sheets still gripped in his hands.

The house in Maryland where the events in the case began.

Those who have come to believe the boy was genuinely possessed feel that he may have been invaded by an invisible entity after experimenting with a talking board, commonly referred to as a "Ouija" board. He had been taught to use the device by his "Aunt Tillie," a relative who took an active interest in Spiritualism and the occult. Tillie had passed away a short time before the events began and it has even been suggested that it was her spirit who began to plague the boy. This seems unlikely, though, especially considering the timing of her death. She lived in St. Louis and had died of multiple sclerosis on January 26, 1949 -- a number of days *after* the phenomena surrounding Robbie began. However, the family did feel there was some connection, as was evidenced in the written history of the mystery -- the so-called "exorcist's diary" that was kept by the Jesuits who were later involved in the case.

As it has turned out, the only details that we have about the case have come from this "diary" and from witnesses who were present at the time. The Catholic Church has never released details of the story. The diary does reveal details, though, many of which have been overlooked and forgotten over the years or which have been ignored to the benefit of whatever agenda was being furthered by each individual author's works. We'll take a closer look at the mystery of the diary, how many pages it may have actually been composed of and just what happened to the various copies of it later on in this book.

As mentioned, the strange noises and scratching in the house progressed into actual witnessed attacks on Robbie himself. The first events occurred on January 15 and were chronicled in the "exorcist's diary." The notation read:

On January 15, 1949, at the home of Roland as he was referred to in the diary , a dripping noise was heard by Roland and his grandmother in the grandmother's bedroom. This noise continued for a short time and then the picture of Christ on the wall shook as if the wall had been bumped. By the time the parents of Roland returned home there was a definite scratching sound under the floorboards near the grandmother's bed. From this night on, the scratching was heard every night about seven o'clock and would continue until midnight. The family thought that the scratching was caused by a rodent of some kind. An exterminator was called in who placed chemicals under the floor boards, but the scratching continued and became more distinct when people stamped the floor.

On January 26, the family received word from St. Louis that Aunt Tillie had died. Robbie, who was very close to the older woman, was devastated by the news. He and Aunt Tillie had spent many hours discussing the spirit world and working with the Ouija Board and it was to this item of comfort that Robbie turned when he heard of her death. He spent hours toying with the planchette and while no one ever recalled just what questions he asked from it, or what answers he received, it is almost certain that he was using the board to try and contact Aunt Tillie.

Around this same time, the scratching sounds described in the diary began to fade. They continued on for a short time and then stopped, although Robbie would report many times that he still heard the noises. After a few days, another mysterious sound began, this time in Robbie's bedroom. He described it as sounding like "squeaking shoes" and it was only heard at night, after he had gone to bed. The squeaking sounds went on for a couple of nights and then the scratching started again.

After night after night of this, Robbie's mother began to worry that the incidents might have something to do with Aunt Tillie and so she decided to attempt to contact her spirit. According to the priest's diary, she asked questions aloud and implored Tillie's spirit, if it was really her, to knock three times and make herself known. Allegedly, Robbie, his mother and his grandmother all felt a wave of air pass over them and then heard three knocks on the floor. Robbie's mother asked again, this time for four knocks and they again came in reply. They were followed by scratching sounds on the bed mattress, which then began to shake and vibrate so hard that it slid off the wooden bed frame and onto the floor. When the shaking stopped, the edges of the bed covers were jerked out from under the mattress and lifted straight up off the surface of the bed "as though held up by starch." When the family touched the stiffened comforter, it collapsed into place and the bed looked normal again.

And while these events must have certainly been chilling, it still seems unlikely -- thanks to the fact that she was not dead when the incidents began -- - that they could have been involved with Aunt Tillie, or her ghost. So, why was Robbie's mother so sure that Aunt Tillie could be involved? She pointed to an occurrence that had taken place a short time before Tillie's death, when the family had gone to visit her at her home. They had driven for a few miles in their automobile when a blanket in the back seat began to curl up under its own power. Then, both Robbie and his mother were drawn together by an invisible force and pushed back against the seat. When they arrived at Aunt Tillie's house, Robbie's father reached for the ignition to shut off the engine but the key had somehow vanished from the switch. It was later found under the front seat. Were these events paranormal and most importantly, were they connected to Aunt Tillie? Robbie's mother believed they were and in the beginning, she was sure that Robbie was being haunted by her ghost.

There are other explanations for what was going on, however. Many believe that Robbie may have been the victim of "poltergeist-like phenomena," where unknowing people actually manifest a form of psychokinesis that causes objects to move about in their presence. Such activity has been well-documented over the years, even if it has not been fully embraced by mainstream science. It usually occurs in cases of troubled young people and can manifest in a variety of ways, including strange sounds, moving objects, knocking and scratching noises and more. This explanation came up several times in the case and some of the principals explored it further, as will become evident later on.

Another explanation, and one offered by more people than you might imagine, was that the boy truly was possessed and that the invisible presence wreaking havoc in the house was not connected to Aunt Tillie at all, but was supernatural - and demonic-- in origin.

No matter what was causing them to occur, the reported events continued. Not all of them were confined to Robbie's home, although most did occur there. There were witnesses to the eerie events that occurred, both at Robbie's school and at home with family and friends, although reports of neighbors hearing "manic screams" and "terrifying noises" coming from the house have been greatly exaggerated. Mark Opsasnick, who thoroughly investigated the portion of the case that occurred in Maryland, spoke to many former neighbors but none of them remembered any odd sounds coming from the house. In fact, it was pretty evenly divided as to whether or not they knew their former neighbor was actually even connected to the "Exorcist Case."

"Robbie Doe" in high school, several years after the events in the case took place.

One of Robbie's neighbors was an old friend, Alvin Kagey, who remembered that the boy had been "sick" and had been taken to St. Louis for "treatment." He was later aware of his friend's connection to the "exorcism," although it was never talked about in town. His information had come from his parents, who had heard about it directly from Robbie's father. Another neighbor, also aware of what was happening to Robbie in 1949, stated that he never believed the boy was possessed. He believed it was a psychological problem. Others in the community were less charitable. One or two described Robbie as a problem child who was smothered by a religious mother and an aunt with an interest in Spiritualism. He was an unpopular loner, they said, shunned by his classmates at school, prone to tantrums and violence toward his family and few friends and was often cruel and sadistic toward other children and even animals. They believed the "possession" was nothing more than a "dysfunctional boy" looking for attention.

But not everyone felt this way. Even the most skeptical had to admit that some of the reports, and the witnesses to the reported activity, gave them pause. These were not sketchy accounts from the back pages of newspapers or gossip passed along by friends. The stories about what was happening to Robbie were first-hand accounts from not only family members and relatives but from ministers, psychologists and priests who wrote down what they witnessed.

And they had strange stories to tell.

In January 1949, Robbie was in the eighth grade at the Bladensburg Junior High School in Maryland. He was removed from class at that time, thanks to several weird events that occurred. The desks at school were movable seat and desk units with a single arm that acted as a writing surface. On several occasions in January and February, Robbie's desk slid into the aisle and began jerking about the classroom, banging into other desks and causing an uproar. Although the teacher understandably assumed that Robbie was pushing the desk around with his feet, Robbie swore that he had not caused it to move. He maintained that it slid across the floor by itself and that there had been nothing that he could do to stop it.

Robbie always seemed to be nearby when anything strange occurred. A book flew out of the bookcase and landed at his feet. A coat flew off the hanger in the closet and draped itself over his shoulder. Items on the kitchen counter vaulted across the room in his direction, clattering onto the floor. The kitchen table lifted on one end and flipped over. Clothing that he had placed on a chair in his bedroom was found scattered on the floor when no one was in the room. And the weird happenings went on and on.

One weekend, a number of relatives came to visit and Robbie was sitting with them in the living room, relaxing in a large, overstuffed chair. Suddenly, the back legs of the chair rose into the air and flipped forward, dumping Robbie out of it. The boy went sprawling onto the floor, dazed and a little shaken. Family members, who were surprised by what they had just seen, gathered around the chair, checking to see if something was wrong with it. Robbie's father and a burly uncle both sat down in the chair and tried to flip it over. Neither one of them could do it.

As they were still examining the chair, one of Robbie's aunts pointed to a small end table near the couch. A vase that had been sitting on the table slowly lifted off of it and seemed to hang in the air for a few moments. With a flash, it shot across the room and smashed against the wall.

One night, the quiet of the house was shattered by screams coming from Robbie's room. His parents and grandmother rushed into the bedroom and as he lay screaming on the bed, they watched a heavy dresser slide across the room, blocking their exit back through the door. The drawers of the dresser began to open and close, sliding out and slamming back in again. This continued for nearly a minute and then stopped.

On another occasion, Robbie's family went to visit some friends, who lived about forty miles away. The afternoon passed uneventfully until Robbie sat down

47

in a rocking chair in the living room. The adults were chatting in the other room when they heard a sharp cry from the boy. They rushed into the room and later agreed that they had all seen the same thing -- the rocking chair, with Robbie sitting in it, spinning around and around in the middle of the room. His feet were well off the floor and the chair seemed to be spinning under its own power. It was impossible for it to be moving in the way that it was, but there was no denying what they had seen with their own eyes.

By this time, the family was becoming desperate. They began seeking help for Robbie and according to one account from 1975, called in two Lutheran ministers and a rabbi. Robbie had been baptized a Lutheran at birth, so one has to wonder why a rabbi was called to the house, although some have suggested that perhaps one of the ministers had asked him along. The account goes on to say that while the rabbi was examining the boy, Robbie suddenly began to shout in an unknown tongue. After listening for a few moments, the rabbi announced that he was speaking in Hebrew. Not only that, but the report adds that a professor from the Catholic University in Washington would later hear the boy's speech and he insisted that Robbie was speaking Aramaic, an ancient language of Palestine. If this account is accurate, we have to ask - how could a thirteen-year-old boy from Maryland learn to speak Aramaic?

But the question remains as to whether either of these reports of Robbie speaking in a foreign language is really accurate. There is nothing in the "exorcist's diary" that suggests that Robbie ever spoke in an unknown tongue which seems to question whether there should have been an exorcism at all, based on the Church's own criteria and this is the only notation of him speaking in tongues during any part of the case. There is nothing in the 1975 account to show where this information came from, so the reader is asked to judge for himself as to whether or not it can be accepted as evidence of the case's authenticity.

In addition to this somewhat apocryphal account, we do have reports that say Robbie's parents sought help from other sources. Robbie was examined by a physician, as well as a psychologist and a psychiatrist. No records are available as to what occurred during these visits, except for a remarks that came from the physician and the psychiatrist. The doctor said that he found nothing wrong with Robbie, although he was "somewhat high-strung." The psychiatrist was more critical, stating that he found Robbie to be "normal" and that "he did not believe the phenomena." He also stated that Robbie was irritated with all of his questions and procedures.

Still worried that all of the strangeness in the house was connected to Aunt Tillie, Robbie's mother also brought in some additional, much stranger, help. This was also noted in the "exorcist's diary":

48

A Spiritualist was called in to use his formulae for ridding people of spirits but he had no success. It should be remarked here that Aunt Tillie believed very much in Spiritualism and often consulted Spiritualists

This was the only mention made of the family trying to seek help from the Spiritualist community, of which Aunt Tillie was a prominent member. However, this did not end Robbie's mother's belief that the activity was somehow connected to her.

Unsure of what to direction in which to turn next, Robbie's parents contacted the pastor of their own Lutheran church, Rev. Luther Schulze. It was natural that the family turned to the Lutheran faith in this time of trouble, even though both Robbie's father and his grandmother had been born into the Catholic Church. His father had never practiced his religion but his grandmother had been a practicing Catholic until she was fourteen years old. There is no indication as to why she did not remain in the Church. Robbie's mother, however, had been born and raised as a Lutheran and was deeply religious. Robbie had been born into the faith and had been baptized when he was six months old.

After the minister was contacted, Schulze came over to the family's home and listened politely to the litany of strange events that were taking place in the house. He was skeptical at first, until he allegedly had the opportunity to see the activity as it was actually occurring. He later stated that he saw furniture move about in the house, pushed by unseen hands. He saw dishes fly through the air, saw glasses break and watched as Robbie's bed vibrated and shook. He first thought that all of it could be dismissed as the work of a clever prankster but soon changed his mind. He became determined to try and help the family however he could.

Schulze was unsure how to deal with what was occurring, especially in light of the new theories being suggested by Robbie's family. They told the minister that while all of the strange happenings were disturbing, they were becoming more unsettled by the changes they were starting to notice in Robbie. He had become very morose and depressed and kept increasingly to himself, barely speaking to anyone. One night, in his sleep, they heard him cursing and using obscenities that they refused to repeat to the minister. His personality was completely different than it had been just weeks before. His parents were convinced that a spirit -- perhaps that of Aunt Tillie -- was haunting their house and has turned its attentions to Robbie. They were now also beginning to wonder about diabolical possession.

Schulze had little knowledge of this phenomenon. As a Lutheran minister, he knew that Martin Luther, who had split off from the Catholic Church and had founded the Lutheran faith, had considered all mental illnesses to be cases of diabolical possession. Of course, in the modern times of the middle twentieth century, enlightened men like Schulze no longer believed this. One of the first recommendations that he gave the family was for them to seek psychiatric help for the boy. He was not equipped to deal with even the possibility of possession since it was no longer part of the theology of the Lutheran Church. Martin Luther had expelled many of the rituals of Catholicism, including the rites of exorcism. He believed that a ritual for casting out demons merely made a "display" of the devil and he preferred to confront the devil with "prayer and contempt."

Schulze tried following Luther's example and began praying with Robbie and his parents in their home and then with Robbie alone. He took the boy to the church to pray with him and he begged whatever was bothering him to leave. It didn't help, however, and the strange manifestations continued. The weird noises continued to be heard in the house and Robbie's bed went on shaking so hard that he was unable to get any sleep at night.

The minister still rejected the idea of demonic possession, though. To him, the idea of a person being possessed by an evil spirit was a Roman Catholic belief. He believed there was a very real explanation for what was taking place and while certainly paranormal, was not the work of any devil. Schulze had long been interested in parapsychology, the study of events that do not seem to be explicable by conventional science. He read everything that he could get his hands on about the subject and believed that extrasensory perception ESP existed in most people in varying degrees. In 1949, experiments with ESP focused on three types of phenomena: telepathy, which was the ability to send thoughts from one person's mind to another; clairvoyance, an ability to perceive events or things that cannot be ordinarily known; and psychokinesis, the movement of physical objects by thought alone.

Schulze was especially interested in psychokinesis PK and from his first involvement with Robbie's family, he suspected that the boy might be unconsciously manipulating the items that were moving about in the house. As mentioned earlier, this ability often manifests in cases of troubled young people and Robbie certainly fit the bill.

The minister kept this theory to himself, though, especially since Robbie's parents were still convinced that their house -- and Robbie himself -- was being haunted. Night after night, Robbie thrashed in his bed for hours, half asleep or in some sort of trance. When he finally went to sleep, he often screamed during horrific nightmares or mumbled incoherent phrases as if he were talking to someone that his parents could not see. They pleaded with Rev. Schulze to try and help their son.

50

Finally, on February 17, Schulze decided to try and ascertain whether the house was haunted, as the parents believed, or whether Robbie was. He knew that if the "haunting," or in this case the paranormal phenomena, was connected to the boy, then it would follow him away from his house. With that in mind, he offered to let Robbie spend the night in his home and his parents quickly agreed. They were anxious to try anything that might help by this time. If nothing else, Robbie might finally manage to get an entire night of sleep.

That night, Mrs. Schulze went to the guest room and Robbie and the minister retired to the twin beds located in the master bedroom. About ten minutes later, Schulze reported that he heard the sound of Robbie's bed creaking and shaking. He also heard strange scratching noises inside of the walls, just like the ones that had been heard at Robbie's own house. Schulze quickly switched on the lights and clearly saw the vibrating bed. When he prayed for it to stop, the vibration grew even more violent. He stated that Robbie was wide awake but he was completely still and was not moving in a way that would cause the bed to shake. The bed was shaking, he later reported, "like one of those motel vibrator beds, but much faster." Robbie was wide awake and completely still. Schulze reported, "His limbs and head and body were perfectly still."

Aside from the prayers that he had offered, Schulze was determined not to react to the bed's movements. He decided to get himself and Robbie out of the room instead. He stood up and speaking calmly, announced that the two of them should go to the kitchen and get some hot cocoa. After making it, they went into the study with the steaming mugs. Robbie politely thanked the minister for the cocoa but said little else. He was quiet and according to Schulze, seemed undisturbed by the activity. He assumed that perhaps Robbie had gotten used to the strange events or --- as he had suspected originally -- that he might be faking them in some way. He watched the boy carefully as they finished their cocoa and then they returned to the bedroom.

Rather than get back into the bed, Schulze suggested that Robbie try and sleep in a heavy armchair that was located across the room. He decided to leave one of the lights on. While Schulze watched him closely, the chair began to move. First, it scooted backward several inches and its legs jolted forward and back. The minister told Robbie to raise his legs and to add his full weight to the chair but that wasn't enough to stop the chair from moving. Moments later, it literally slammed against the wall and then it tipped over and deposited the boy unhurt onto the floor.

Schulze guessed that it had taken more than a minute for the chair to slowly tip over and dump Robbie out of it. Robbie never moved in the chair and appeared to be in some sort of trance. The minister had been standing in front of the chair when all of this occurred. When Robbie fell onto the floor, he stepped around the boy and sat down in the chair himself. Robbie slowly wandered away as the minister tried to tip the chair over himself. The heavy armchair had "a very low center of gravity," he reported, and he was unable to knock it over.

Trying not to be frightened or discouraged, Rev. Schulze made a pallet of blankets on the floor for Robbie to sleep on. He left the same light burning and tried to settle the boy down to sleep. Robbie soon drifted off and a few minutes later, the minister nodded off as well. He woke up around 3:00 a.m. and caught movement out of the corner of his eye. When he looked, he realized that he was seeing Robbie's pallet sliding across the floor. The boy and the blankets moved slowly under one of the beds and Schulze realized that the four sides of the blanket, which had no folds, remained perfectly straight as it seemed to float across the wood floor. If someone had been pushing them, they would have wrinkled. But he refused to believe what he was seeing and so Schulze finally shouted at Robbie to stop moving the makeshift bed.

When Robbie was startled awake, he raised up and struck his head on the iron springs under the bed. Stiff and still acting as though he was in a trance, Robbie never even flinched as his head and face slammed into the springs over and over again.

After this active night, Schulze was now both puzzled and a little afraid. If Schulze still believed that Robbie was faking the activity, then that belief was certainly shattered by what he had seen. He questioned Robbie's parents about their visits to physicians and psychologists to rule out any kind of physical and mental problems that might be causing the phenomena to take place. The minister also contacted J.B. Rhine, the famed founder of the parapsychology laboratory at Duke University. He explained what was going on and Rhine and his partner and wife, Louisa Rhine, drove up from North Carolina to see the boy. Unfortunately, no activity took place while the investigator was present, but Rhine did deduce that it sounded like a classic poltergeist case in which the boy's unconscious abilities were influencing the objects around him. The details fit well with other experimental results that Rhine had been obtaining.

And while the explanation suggested by Rhine appealed to the minister, largely thanks to his own interest in the field, he did an abrupt about-face a short time later when the phenomena surrounding Robbie took another turn.

As he had been since the beginning of the case, Robbie seemed perfectly normal during the daytime hours. At night, however, he was anything but calm. His sleep was still traumatized by horrible nightmares and the scratching sounds continued coming from inside of the walls. His mattress vibrated and rocked and he was constantly awakened by the noises and movements. Then, on February 26, strange marks began to appear on Robbie's body.

They appeared to be scratches, long and shallow furrows that looked like bloody marks that had left behind by a cat's claws. They appeared on Robbie's arms, legs and chest and some of them seemed to be letters of the alphabet. They were letters but they did form any words ---- not yet anyway.

Perhaps startled by this new turn of events, Rev. Schulze realized that what he had been doing was not enough to stop what was happening to Robbie. He suggested that Robbie's family contact a Catholic priest. "You have to see a Catholic priest," the parents recalled him saying. "The Catholics know about things like this."

And after this, things get if possible even more confusing.

The story gets so convoluted at this point because of the alternate versions of history that have been reported to occur between February 26 and the early days of March when Robbie and his family departed Maryland for St. Louis. The alternate versions of the story include a dramatic, widely accepted version and a more mundane although still troubling version that is much more likely to be the truth.

Let's take a look at the more exciting version of the story first:

According to some sources, Robbie's family turned to the Catholic Church on the recommendation of Rev. Schulze. His father called the rectory of St. James, a Catholic church near their home, and asked to speak with a priest. Father E. Albert Hughes, a young priest who was the assistant pastor at the church at the time, was called to the telephone. He was skeptical and reluctant to get involved in the matter, but he did suggest that Robbie's father stop by the rectory the following morning.

Father Hughes listened patiently to the longer version of the story that he was given the next day but he offered little in the way of assistance. He promised to pray for Robbie and his gave his father a bottle of holy water and some blessed candles. He told Robbie's father to sprinkle the holy water around the boy's room and to put the candles there and light them whenever anything unusual happened.

Robbie's father took the holy water and candles home with him and gave the items to his wife. Later on that evening, she opened the bottle of holy water, sprinkling every room. She then placed the bottle on a dresser in Robbie's room and placed the candles next to them. She lit them and hoped for the best -- but they did nothing to dampen the activity. Robbie's mother reported that, during the night, the bottle was picked up by an unseen force and smashed. She also stated that she had lit one of the candles, only to have the flame shoot all of the way up to the ceiling. She snuffed it out but was too afraid to light any of the other candles for fear that they would burn down the house.

According to the story, Father Hughes told her to try again and she hung up the telephone. She called back a few minutes later and the priest heard a loud crashing sound on the other end of the line. According to Robbie's mother, the telephone table in the house had just shattered into dozens of pieces.

After this, Father Hughes decided to go to the house and talk to Robbie so that he could get an idea of what was going on. During the visit, Robbie allegedly addressed the priest in Latin, a language that he did not know. It was said that this incident was what started Hughes thinking that Robbie could be possessed. This is the second time that Robbie was reported to have spoken in a foreign tongue and but once again, nothing of this incident appears in the "exorcist's diary". It was passed along to author Thomas Allen from a friend of Father Hughes, making it third-hand information at best. Based on some of the other information contained in this version of events, this may be just more of the erroneous history contained here. The reader can judge this for himself when he discovers the rest of the evidence.

Shaken by Robbie's outburst, Hughes was said to have applied to his archbishop, the Most Reverend Patrick A. O'Boyle, for permission to conduct an exorcism. According to Hughes, he first went to O'Boyle's aide, the chancellor of the archdioceses, who advised Hughes to go slowly with the case. But Father Hughes was convinced by this time and he insisted that he was ready to move forward. The chancellor relented and made an appointment for Hughes to see O'Boyle.

The Most Reverend Patrick O'Boyle was a protégé of the most powerful Catholic official in America at the time, Frances Cardinal Spellman, the archbishop of New York. O'Boyle was born to an Irish immigrant family in 1896 and after his father's death when he was only ten, his mother became a housekeeper at a church rectory. O'Boyle grew up wanting to emulate the men that his mother worked for and he entered the seminary as soon as he was old enough. When he was ordained, he was assigned to the New York archdiocese and was recognized by Spellman, then a Bishop, as an energetic young priest. When Spellman became the Archbishop in 1939, he took O'Boyle under his wing. He served Spellman during World War II and in 1947, when the archbishop of Baltimore and Washington died, the Vatican divided the jurisdiction, creating archdioceses for both cities. O'Boyle, then in New York as the executive director of Catholic Charities, was made the archbishop of the new archdiocese of Washington. It was the first time that a monsignor, O'Boyle's station at the time, was appointed as an archbishop in America without having served as a bishop first. On January 14, 1948, Spellman consecrated O'Boyle in St. Patrick's

Cathedral in New York and a few days later, he moved to Washington to take over his post.

Archbishop O'Boyle would certainly make a powerful and influential character in the drama of this case -- but unfortunately, there is not a single record to say that he ever even heard of Robbie's situation, or that he ever met with Father Albert Hughes. The only claim that the two men ever had a meeting appears in an "unpublished, third-hand account" that states that the Archbishop authorized Hughes to begin the exorcism of Robbie. Because an exorcism is supposed to be carried out by a man who has no sin that can be exposed by the demon, Hughes went to Baltimore, where he gave a general confession. A "general confession" differs from an ordinary confession in that it causes the priest to deeply examine his life and find his weaknesses and then confess them to a priest who is designated to hear the confessions of other priests. A general confession would prepare a priest for an event like an exorcism in the same way that a knight would have girded himself with armor before a battle.

There has been a lot of skepticism expressed about this portion of the case because many people with knowledge of the intricacy of exorcisms find it hard to believe that Archbishop O'Boyle would have assigned Robbie's exorcism to someone as inexperienced as Father Hughes. He fit none of the criteria detailed in the last chapter for an exorcist and for this reason, there were many theologians better suited for the task at Washington's Catholic University or Trinity College. O'Boyle could have also called upon the theological and psychological faculties at Georgetown University, a Jesuit institution. Father Hughes had a cursory knowledge of demonology and was a young man who had studied to be a priest, not an exorcist. He was an assistant pastor who had studied the tenets of Catholic theology. He should have been dealing with questions of faith and morals brought to him by ordinary people and not the nightmare of demonic possession. There was nothing in his past that would prepare Father Hughes for an exorcism but in the winter of 1949, he allegedly found himself getting ready to perform one.

Or at least that's one version of the story. According to this account, O'Boyle told Hughes not to write anything down about the exorcism and never to talk about it. For those who have doubts about the story, believers point to these instructions as to why no written record of the meeting between the assistant pastor and the Archbishop exists.

While this was going on, Robbie was getting worse and worse. He was no longer going to school and his daytime hours were filled with fitful naps and long periods when he sat and simply stared out the window. The weird sounds came every night and the red scratches began to appear almost as soon as the sun went down. When he managed to sleep at night, he tossed and turned restlessly and was plagued by more horrific nightmares.

Father Hughes decided to carry out Robbie's exorcism at Georgetown Hospital, part of the Jesuit's Georgetown University - Georgetown University Medical School complex in Washington. According to the account, Hughes got Robbie admitted on his own and did so without the knowledge of an attending physician. Another version of this same account claims that Robbie was admitted by a psychiatrist, who summoned Hughes when Robbie took a turn for the worse. And still another variation claims that the Catholic hospital was well aware that an exorcism was going to take place.

The report continued to say that Robbie was checked into the hospital some time between February 27 and March 4 under an assumed name. The mother superior of the nuns issued strict orders that no records were to be kept of the exorcism. Hughes ordered that Robbie be strapped to the bed since he had no assistants to control the boy if he became violent. Robbie lay on his back with his eyes closed and what happened next depends on what version of this story that you care to believe. The stories include:

Father Hughes entered the room wearing a doctor's gown over his surplice and cassock and Robbie, in a powerful voice that was not his own, ordered Hughes to remove a cross in the room that could not be seen from his position on the bed.

A nun entered the hospital room with a tray and it suddenly flew out of her hands and smashed against the wall.

At one point, as the exorcism was beginning, the hospital bed rolled all of the way across the room on its own and slammed into the wall. The bed shook and jumped and the staff members present were unable to make it be still.

After the exorcism began, Robbie thrashed and jerked on the bed and when confronted with holy water, he began to swear in Aramaic.

These were just some of the stories told about the initial exorcism and as the reader will soon find, it's unlikely that any of them ever occurred.

The most popular incident connected to what has become known as Robbie's "botched exorcism" took place just as Father Hughes was beginning the prayers from the *Rituale Romanum*. He knelt beside Robbie's bed and focused his attention on the prayer books in his hands. As this was occurring, Robbie managed to slip one of his hands out of the straps that held him into place and it disappeared under the bed. Somehow, the boy worked a piece of the bedspring loose and he slashed the priest with it. Hughes screamed and struggled to his feet, his left arm hanging limp at his side. Blood gushed from a wound that ran from his shoulder to his wrist and it required more than one hundred stitches to close it.

Needless to say, this ended the exorcism and Hughes never attempted to finish it. The account states that he subsequently left St. James and suffered a nervous breakdown. Many years later, one of his former parishioners saw him preaching at a church located elsewhere in the archdiocese. During the mass, he could only hold the consecrated host aloft in one hand -- his right hand. Those who knew him say that he was haunted and withdrawn and was simply never the same after the incident at the Georgetown Hospital.

That was the most popular --- and definitely the most exciting --- version of the story. However, according to research done by Mark Opsasnick in 1999, which I confirmed on my own three years later, none of this ever happened at all.

The story of the "Hughes Exorcism" appears only in the book *Possessed* by Thomas Allen. There are a number of other suppositions and possible problems in the book but this is definitely one of the most prominent. The stories about Father Hughes turned out to be almost totally inaccurate. Father Hughes became assistant pastor of St. James Church under Rev. William Canning in June 1948 and he served without a break until June 1960. He was later reassigned to St. James in 1973 and stayed there until his death in 1980. Church records do not indicate that he ever suffered a breakdown, or that he ever made an attempt to exorcize Robbie at Georgetown University Hospital. However, Robbie was checked into the hospital under his real name for several days during the period when the alleged exorcism attempt took place, but that is all. Records say that he underwent extensive medical and psychological evaluations between Monday, February 28 and Thursday, March 3.

Father Hughes also never actually visited Robbie in his home. In truth, his mother brought him to St. James for their only consultation. There is nothing to suggest that Robbie spoke to the priest in Latin or Aramaic and no evidence to say that Father Hughes was ever slashed with a bedspring. Those who knew Hughes personally remember him suffering no injuries during this period and the fact is, the church social calendar showed him quite busy during the weeks after Robbie's release from the hospital. He spoke at seminars, held several masses, and even performed a number of weddings between March and June of 1949 -- the same time that he was allegedly in a mental hospital and or suffering from his serious injury. The local newspaper provided many reports of

Father Hughes' activity from 1949 until his departure from St. James in 1960. The popular priest had performed 2,712 baptisms, 486 marriages, 251 baptisms of converts and 247 burials during his assignment.

It's possible that the confusion about Hughes' part in the case came from the assistant pastor that he had later in life. According to this pastor, Frank Bober, Hughes confided in him about the first exorcism attempt. Bober later became an important figure in the case, being very accessible to journalists. He has appeared in literally dozens of articles, books and documentaries about the case and Thomas Allen cited him as being "extremely reliable" about Hughes' role in the incidents. Others believe that Bober "dramatized" many of the re-tellings of the events and created much of the confusion that surrounds this part of the case. This may certainly be the case.

But even if we consider the idea that this part of the story didn't actually happen, what was documented as actually occurring around this same time was strange enough that all of that becomes almost irrelevant.

Robbie's hospital stay was documented as occurring between February 28, 1949 and March 3, 1949 but according to the "exorcist's diary," strange things began to happen on February 26. The statement records that:

On February 26, 1949, there appeared scratches on the boy's body for about four successive nights. After the fourth night, words were written in printed form. These letters were clear but seemed to have been scratched on the body by claws.

At about this same time, Robbie's mother began to suggest that perhaps a trip away from Maryland might free the boy from the strange happenings. She thought that perhaps they could leave their troubles behind by visiting St. Louis. Robbie's mother was a native of the city and still had many relatives there. The more she considered this, the better the idea seemed. And apparently, the haunting entity agreed because the word "LOUIS" inexplicably appeared on Robbie's rib cage. When this "skin branding" occurred, Robbie's hands were always visible and his mother specifically notes that he could not have scratched the words himself. He had been under observation at the time and the words, according to witnesses, had simply appeared.

The priest's diary even noted that the writing also appeared on Robbie's back. Later on, while in St. Louis, there was some question raised about sending Robbie to school while in the city but the message "NO" appeared on his wrists. A large letter "N" also appeared on each of his legs and his mother feared disobeying what she saw as a supernatural order. It has been suggested that perhaps Robbie created the writing himself with his mind, either consciously or unconsciously. With that in question, it should be noted that before his parents consulted a priest, they also had him examined by a psychiatrist. He reported that the boy was quite normal, as did a medical doctor who gave him a complete physical.

At this point, records do indicate that Robbie's mother took him to consult with Father Hughes at the St. James Church. During this one documented visit, he suggested that the family use blessed candles, holy water and special prayers and to perhaps rid the boy of his problems. Robbie's mother began the use of the blessed candles and on one occasion, a comb flew violently through the air and struck them, snuffing out the flames. The other activity, like the scratching sounds and odd noises, reportedly continued in the family home. According to the "exorcist's diary":

The mother took the bottle of holy water and sprinkled all of the rooms. When she placed the bottle on a shelf the bottle flew across the room but did not break. When she held the lighted candle alongside of Roland ffiRobbieffi at night the whole bed, mother and son moved back and forth with the swaying of the mattress..."

A 1975 report stated that attempts were also made to baptize Robbie into the Catholic faith in order to help him. The press mentioned that one of these attempts was made during Robbie's hospital stay not an exorcism, as was later reported and then later in St. Louis. One baptism attempt was allegedly made in February 1949. It was said that as Robbie's uncle was driving him to the rectory for the ceremony, the boy suddenly glared at him, grabbed him by the throat and shouted, "You son of a bitch, you think I'm going to be baptized but you are going to be fooled!"

The Catholic baptism ritual usually only takes about fifteen minutes but for Robbie, it reportedly lasted for several hours. It was said that when the priest asked "Do you renounce the devil and all his works?" Robbie would go into such a thrashing rage that he had to be restrained.

As mentioned, Robbie was released from the hospital on March 3. During that time, a strange incident took place that I learned of almost by accident from a source who grew up in the Washington, D.C. area. In the summer of 1982, a friend's father told him about one of the most frightening incidents of his life. It had occurred in 1949 in the old infirmary at Georgetown. There had been an outbreak of flu that year and most of the twelve to fifteen year-old boys in the neighborhood including the witness were moved to the infirmary for observation.

My correspondent explained: "He said that one night, around 9:00 p.m., two doctors and a boy who looked about thirteen walked into the room that he and a number of boys were housed in. Needless to say, my friend's father, as well as the other boys, knew nothing about this boy. My friend's father said that he looked directly at the boy, as did the other boys. He said that the boy glared into his eyes. He said that at that moment he was terrified and that some of the boys began saying aloud the Lord's Prayer and Hail Mary. He said that he was so frightened by the boy's eyes that he could not sleep for many nights. He said that after about five minutes, the boy and the doctors left the room. My friend's father said to me that he found out about a year later that the boy was the one who was possessed by the devil and that the boy was held over night in the infirmary before being moved to St. Louis."

PART 2:

THE DEVIL CAME TO ST. LOUIS

During the course of the fifteen minutes of activity a sharp pain seemed to have struck Roland on his stomach and he cried out. The mother quickly pulled back the bed covers and lifted the boy's pajama top enough to show zigzag scratches in bold red lines on the boy's abdomen.
From The "Exorcist's Diary", a case study kept by the Jesuits in the 1949 case

On Saturday, March 5, shortly after being discharged from the hospital and being pronounced "normal" again, Robbie boarded a train to St. Louis with his parents. The family was graciously taken in by relatives in Bel-Nor, which is located on the northwest side of the greater St. Louis area. Here, the boy's mother hoped that he might be freed from the strange and horrifying events. For those readers who are convinced that nothing was occurring in this case aside from overactive imaginations and silly superstition, they may want to consider the trip to St. Louis itself as evidence that something strange supernatural or not was taking place. The fact that Robbie's parents would uproot the boy from his home, his father would travel back and forth, jeopardizing his employment and they would all travel halfway across the county in a last ditch effort to find help is suggestive if not downright convincing that terrible things were indeed happening.

The relatives' home in Bel-Nor as it looks today. It was at this house in the North St. Louis suburb where the exorcism actually began.

The only thing dividing Robbie's relatives in St. Louis was religion. Some of them were Catholic and some of them were Lutheran, but all of them loved Robbie and his parents and wanted to do anything they could to help. They spent their first night in Normandy another St. Louis suburb near Bel-Nor , at the home of a sister of Robbie's mother. They were a Lutheran family and had spoken to their minister in advance of the family's arrival. Their minister did not even take the initiative of Rev. Schulze. He demurred from getting involved in the case at all and suggested, as Schulze did, that the family talk to a Catholic priest.

Any hope that Robbie's troubles had stayed behind in Maryland was dashed on that first night. A heavy bed moved about three feet under its own power at one point in the evening and Robbie himself was afflicted by one of the mysterious "skin brandings." According to the "exorcist's diary":

... writing appeared on Roland's body while he was reading a comic book. There was sharp pain. The writing was done through his clothes. When Roland retired there was violent shaking of the bed and scratching on the mattress. Hardly any relief through the night.

As noted in the diary, it was a fitful night for everyone, especially Robbie, who slept sporadically and when awake, was strangely calm. All of those present

62

in the house were exhausted and for Robbie's relatives, it was their first chance to see the phenomena that they had only heard about until that point. It's apparent that they were terrified. The strange happenings, combined with the warnings from their Lutheran minister, must have convinced them to move Robbie from the house. There is no way that we can know what took place in Normandy, but what we do know is that on Tuesday, March 8, Robbie and his family moved to the home of Robbie's uncle, his father's brother, in nearby Bel-Nor.

The house, located in the 8400 block of Roanoke Drive, was occupied by Robbie's uncle, his aunt and two cousins. One of them, a young boy, was about Robbie's age and his sister was a student at St. Louis University, a Catholic institution. Like his brother, Robbie's uncle was born into the Catholic Church but was not a practicing Catholic. He had married in the Church to satisfy his wife's family and was allowed to do so on the condition that their children be raised Catholic. Like the family of Robbie's mother, they had heard everything about Robbie's ordeal so far. They also knew that his mother's side of the family had called in a Lutheran minister to help but that he had suggested that they speak to a priest about diabolical possession. In spite of any trepidation that they might have been experiencing, they were happy to open their home to the boy.

That afternoon passed with relative calm. Robbie seemed content and happy to see his aunt and uncle. When his cousin came home from school, the two boys played together all afternoon and even dinner passed without incident. After cleaning up the kitchen, and sending the boys off to play, the four adults sat down together and began discussing the situation. After an entire day that was free of the strange happenings, Robbie's parents began to consider making his stay in St. Louis a lengthy one. His mother asked her sister-in-law about the possibility of enrolling Robbie at his cousin's school.

Almost as soon as she said this, the adults heard Robbie let out a sharp cry from the other room. When his mother walked into the room, he was looking at her coldly, almost with an expression on anger on his face. Then, he grimaced and flinched and slowly lifted the bottom of his shirt. As mentioned in the last chapter, the words "NO SCHOOL" could be seen scratched into chest. The word "NO" would also later appear on his wrists and on his legs. His parents, filled with fear, never mentioned the idea of Robbie starting school in St. Louis again.

Later on that night, Robbie went to bed in his cousin's room. The boys, who had spent many overnight visits with one another over the years, seemed fine as their parents tucked them in and aside from some giggling and horsing around, nothing occurred for the first hour or so. Their parents were breathing a sigh of relief when strange sounds started coming from the bedroom, followed by a yelp of surprise from Robbie's cousin.

The four adults rushed into the bedroom and heard weird scratching sounds coming from the mattress the boys were laying on. The boys were on their backs on the bed, frightened but motionless, as the mattress furiously slammed up and down. The bed itself lurched back and forth, sliding forward across the room. Robbie's cousin would later report that he had seen a stool that was sitting near the bed go flying across the room a few seconds before the mattress started moving.

Needless to say, Robbie's aunt and uncle were terrified, as was his cousin, but to Robbie's parents, it was more of the same thing they had been experiencing in Maryland. They were completely at a loss as to what to do now. Fortunately, though, Robbie's older cousin had an idea of her own. As mentioned, she was enrolled at St. Louis University and when she heard about what had happened in her brother's bedroom, she suggested that she speak to one of her Jesuit teachers at the university. Robbie's parents agreed and for what was truly the first time aside from some prayers and suggestions from Father Hughes , the Catholic Church was brought into the case.

The next day, Robbie's cousin arranged a meeting with her favorite teacher, Father Raymond J. Bishop, S.J., the forty-three-year-old head of the Department of Education and a superb instructor of prospective teachers, which Robbie's cousin planned to be. Father Bishop was regarded as a good listener, a genial man and popular instructor who always had time for his students. He was also known for having a quality that was possessed by many other members of the Society of Jesus, the Jesuits, he was a devout man who never acted pious or better than anyone else.

Bishop listened carefully to everything that the young woman told him, from the incidents in Maryland to the strange happenings that had occurred over the course of just two days while Robbie was in St. Louis. Her concerns were not only for Robbie but for her own family too. She also told him of the opinions expressed by the Lutheran ministers about Robbie possibly being possessed.

Whatever Bishop thought of the strange stories, he kept his opinions to himself. If Robbie was truly possessed, there were certain signs that he would have to see for himself. He would need to see the boy but he would also have to confer with other Jesuits as well. He told Robbie's cousin that he took her account very seriously and that he would get back with her as soon as possible.

Father Bishop then sought out Father Laurence J. Kenny, S.J., another Jesuit who was well-known for his warmth and wisdom. Kenney was in his nineties by this time and had just recently retired as a professor of history. He was a confessor to many of the priests in the Jesuit community and Bishop knew that he had been around long enough to have experience just about everything imaginable. After hearing what Bishop had been told by Robbie's cousin, Kenny could understand the concerns about the boy being possessed. He urged a meeting with Father Paul Reinert, S.J., president of St. Louis University.

The case of Robbie Doe was now firmly in the hands of the Jesuits -- and it could not be in a better place.

The Jesuits were formerly known as the Society of Jesus. The society has long been considered the intellectual arm of the Catholic Church and over the centuries has often been at odds with the more conservative elements of the Church. The Society of Jesus was founded in 1540 by St. Ignatius Loyola and since then has grown to more than 24,000 members in 112 countries. Loyola was a Spanish Basque soldier who underwent an extraordinary conversion while recovering from a cannon ball wound that occurred during battle. He wrote about his religious experiences, which he called "Spiritual Exercises," and later founded the Society of Jesus with the approval of Pope Paul III. Over the last several centuries, a number of Jesuits have become renowned for their sanctity and their scholarship in every conceivable field of study, from exploration to scientific discovery, and have especially become known for their work in education.

From the beginning, the Jesuits provided the Church with outstanding men, including doctors in Europe and missionaries to almost every part of the world. They led the Counter Reformation in Europe and missionaries assisted Catholics in England who suffered under the terrible Elizabethan persecutions. Scores of them were killed in the prisons of great cities, while others died in the forests, deserts and jungles of distant lands. No other Catholic order has more martyrs to the faith and no order can claim as many members who have spent time in jail.

Ignatius Loyola had gathered around him an energetic band of well-educated men who desired nothing more than to help others find God in their lives. His original plan had been to form a society of roving missionaries but it soon became clear that colleges offered the greatest possible service to the church, offering moral and religious instruction, as well as teaching the Gospel of service. The new Jesuit schools that formed became such an influential party of the Catholic reform that it was later called "a rebirth of the infant church." The genius and innovation that the Jesuits brought to education came from Loyola's "Spiritual Exercises," the object of which was to free a person from predisposition and bias, thus enabling free choice and a happy and fulfilled life.

The Jesuits were always deeply involved in scholarship, in science and exploration. By 1750, thirty of the world's astronomical observatories were overseen by Jesuit astronomers and thirty-five lunar craters have been named to honor Jesuit astronomers. The Gregorian calendar system was the work of Jesuit Christopher Clavius, the "most influential teacher of the Renaissance." Five of the eight major rivers in the world were first charted by Jesuit explorers. Two of the statues in Statuary Hall in the United States Capitol Building in Washington are Jesuits: Eusebio Kino and Jacques Marquette.

Spanish Jesuits went to Paraguay in 1607, built settlements which lasted from 1607 to 1767 for the indigenous people and taught them how to govern and defend themselves against the Spanish slave traders. They also taught agriculture, architecture, metallurgy, farming, music, ranching and printing. These natives of Paraguay were printing books on art, literature as well as school texts in these settlements before the American Revolution. This society was eventually crushed by the influential slave traders, who were able to intimidate the Spanish crown into destroying the settlements. King Charles III expelled the Jesuits in 1767. The settlements that they had helped to create were called "a triumph of humanity" by Voltaire and one has to wonder what the history of Latin America would have been like if the settlements had been allowed to continue.

The Jesuits were known as the "schoolmasters of Europe" during the sixteenth, seventeenth and eighteenth centuries, not only because of their schools and universities but also for their acclaim as scholars and for the thousands of textbooks that they composed. The Jesuits were largely responsible for an explosion of intellectual activity in Europe with books, scientific study and more than seven hundred schools.

But all of this was lost in 1773. The Jesuits had made many powerful enemies over the years, as was evidenced by their earlier expulsion from Paraguay. In 1773, the entire society was disbanded on orders from the Pope himself. Pope Clement XIV, yielding to pressure from the Bourbon Courts, fearing the loss of the Papal States and anticipating that other European countries might follow the example of Henry VIII who abandoned the Catholic Church and took his whole country with him , issued his brief *Dominus ac Redemptor,* which suppressed the Society of Jesus. The order was disbanded and the property of the Society's schools was sold off. Their libraries were broken up and the books were either burned, sold or taken away by those who had collaborated in the suppression. As if unsure of the justness of the suppression, the Pope promulgated the brief in an unusual manner, which caused perplexing canonical difficulties. Whenever a papal edict was passed, the edict was "promulgated", or publicly made known, so that there was no question as to the legality of it. In the case of the Jesuit suppression, the brief was so badly handled that Catherine, Empress of Russia, rejected it outright. Because of this, two hundred Jesuits continued to function in Russia for many years after the Society was destroyed.

Forty-one years passed before the Society was restored by Pope Pius VII. Although many of the Jesuits who had seen their dreams destroyed had died by that time, the memory of their educational triumphs had not. The new Society was soon flooded with requests for them to take over colleges, including eighty-six in France alone. Since 1814, when the order was restored, the Society has experienced amazing growth and has since surpassed the early Society in its educational, intellectual and pastoral endeavors.

Father Bishop and Father Kenny made an appointment to see Father Reinert within days of hearing about Robbie's ordeal from his cousin. Unfortunately for the university president, a case of possible possession could not have come at a worse time. He was greatly concerned about whether or not the situation would prove to be an embarrassment for St. Louis University. Thanks to his hard work, he believed the university was currently playing an important role in an effort on the part of many American Jesuits to take the Society into a new era.

Reinert's campus housed the controversial Institute of Social Order, a liberal "think tank" that had been founded by the Jesuits against the counsel of critics in Rome and it was working for something that was largely disregarded by many in the general public in those days, including many Catholic parishioners. Jesuits from the Institute of Social Order had been working hard to desegregate the city of St. Louis. The Jesuits had four black parishes in the city, as well as all-black schools, employment bureaus, summer camps and a retreat house. Tempers had flared over the issue and Reinert's predecessor had angrily expelled the most outspoken Jesuit in the community. In 1944, though, St. Louis University had been the first educational institution in Missouri to integrate. Three years later, the Most Reverend Joseph Ritter, Archbishop of St. Louis, desegregated the archdiocese. Many saw this as the Jesuits "pushing" the archbishop into desegregation.

The history of the Jesuit Order shows that it stands as an unusual element in the Catholic Church. For this reason, the Jesuits are used to operating outside of the Catholic hierarchy of pope to bishop to pastor. The Jesuit hierarchy is made up of only Jesuits. Each province operates under a Father Provincial, who reports to the Superior General in Rome, who is under the authority of the Pope. Historically, the Jesuits have often clashed with the Vatican and because of these conflicts, the black-robed Superior General has often been referred to as the "Black Pope."

In 1949, though, the Jesuits and the Vatican were at peace with one another. But, as it had always been, the Jesuits stood alone. Many American Jesuits were thought of as having more faith in themselves than in the central authority in Rome and in having more interest in the matters of this world than of the next.

The Catholic Church in America is formed around the parish, an area that usually coincides with a secular neighborhood. The pastor of the parish is under the supervision of a bishop, or often in large cities, an archbishop. Jesuit communities at institutions like St. Louis University were under dual control. The Father Provincial governs the Jesuits and their activities in his province, while the bishop or archbishop governs the activities of the Jesuit priests. Without his permission, they cannot perform marriages, cannot say Mass, offer Holy Communion or even preside over a Catholic funeral under his authority.

This presented Reinert with a problem. If Father Bishop's story was true and this turned out to be a case of demonic possession, then Reinert would have to deal with Archbishop Ritter on the matter of an exorcism. Permission would have to be granted to the Jesuits and Reinert was not sure that he wanted to broach the subject at such a volatile time. There was an uneasy truce between the university and the archdiocese and while the churches had been desegregated, the Jesuits were still at work trying to get the city desegregated too. While Ritter was in favor of desegregation, he might not necessarily be in favor of the attention that the Jesuits were bringing to the Church. He wondered what effect an exorcism might have on the Jesuit's relationship with Ritter. And he also wondered what the public might think about the Jesuits, who wanted black people treated equally in St. Louis, resurrecting "superstitious nonsense" like an exorcism in these modern times.

As it happened, the Society of Jesus had recently changed the responsibilities of presidents of Jesuit universities. They had once also been rectors, responsible for the well-being of both the university and the Jesuit community, but now another Jesuit was the rector and Reinert's position had become more of an administrative one. He now had no direct responsibility for what was a spiritual problem. If there was to be an exorcism, then Father Bishop would have to apply for permission from Archbishop Ritter himself. This allowed Reinert to stay out of direct contact with the matter. However, he did agree to meet with Bishop and Kenny and according to Father Bishop, he discussed the matter with them at great length.

Father Bishop did not record what Reinert said to him but he did advise him not to go into the situation blindly. He suggested that Bishop go to the house, offer a "priestly blessing" and find out for himself what was going on. After that, he could get back in touch with Reinert and they would decide what to do next.

It should be mentioned at this point that Father Bishop had already gone above and beyond what he was required to do in the case. In that initial discussion with Robbie's cousin about the boy's situation, Bishop and the rest of the Jesuit community came to the decision that they were duty-bound to solve the problem.

Bishop could have easily told the cousin, a practicing Catholic, that she should go and speak to a priest in her parish but he did not. The Jesuits felt they had a spiritual responsibility to help the girl, and help Robbie as well. Bishop was determined to see the thing through to the end.

Father Raymond Bishop was born to German immigrants in Glencoe, Minnesota and attended parochial school before going on to the secular Glencoe Public High School. After graduation, he decided to become a teacher and enrolled in a year-long training program, which he completed with high honors. He spent the next year teaching in rural Minnesota schools but for some reason, chose not to stay with it. After the first year, he entered the University of Minnesota to be become a pharmacist but he would not stay on this course either. While in college, he decided to change his life and become a Jesuit.

Bishop entered the Society of Jesus in 1927 and took up a spiritual system of discipline and studies that had changed little since the days of St. Ignatius Loyola. After a few months of probation, he began a two-year novitiate devoted to prayer and meditation with humbling menial chores. He lived in silence each day, paced by bells that called him to Mass, to meditation, classes, meals and everything else that he did each day. At the end of the two years, he took vows of obedience, chastity and poverty and then was allowed to add "S.J." after his name.

Bishop then spent the next eleven years in study at the St. Stanislaus Seminary near Florissant, Missouri, a small town on the outskirts of St. Louis. He studied Greek and Latin for two years and then philosophy for the next three. All of his classes were in Latin, as were the debates that were staged to test the student's knowledge and his ability to think quickly. Bishop lived a life of study, isolation and humility and only left the seminary after his seventh year, when he was assigned a teaching position at the Jesuit high school operated by St. Louis University. He then spent four years in theology classes and at the end of his third year, was ordained as a Jesuit priest. By this time, Bishop had been in the society for thirteen years and he began a sort of internship that was devoted to priestly, rather than scholarly, work.

At the end of Bishop's "formation" period, he was assigned to Rockhurst College in Kansas City, where became the dean of the College of Arts and Sciences. This position was short-lived, however, when the director of the Department of Education at St. Louis University became gravely ill. Bishop was ordered to St. Louis to assist the man but he died soon after and Bishop took over the position. He had been the head of the department for almost seven years when the case of Robbie Doe was brought to him by a worried and scared young woman.

On the morning following his meeting with Reinert, Father Bishop called Robbie's cousin and told her that he wanted to see the boy as soon as possible. On the evening of March 9, a member of the family picked up Bishop at the university and drove him to their home on Roanoke Drive.

It was a cool, quiet evening when Father Bishop arrived at the two-story brick house in suburban Bel-Nor. Robbie's cousin introduced Bishop to her parents and then led him into the front room so that he could meet Robbie's parents. They quickly warmed up to the kind, compassionate priest and began telling him what had been happening to their son. Bishop questioned them cautiously, looking for any inconsistencies in their story, and taking pages of notes. They told him about Aunt Harriet, the Ouija Board that Robbie had obsessively used after his aunt's death and the bizarre happenings that had occurred in their home. They told him of what had happened with Rev. Schulze in Maryland but never mentioned any abortive exorcism with Father Hughes -- further evidence of the fact that this incident likely never actually took place.

After speaking with the parents for quite some time, Father Bishop then sat down alone with Robbie. He found him to be, according to his account, a quiet boy and one who was not very athletic. Robbie was fond of comic books but otherwise was not much of a reader. He was intelligent but Bishop understood that he was usually bored with school and did not excel at his studies. He was, no matter what else, not the type of boy who made trouble for his parents. The priest was able to base this on his past experience working with young people, not only at St. Louis University but also at the high school that was run by the university. He had taught at the school for some time and encountered many boys like Robbie. He was socially introverted, Bishop believed, but not a troublemaker, which is why what Robbie's parents told him bothered him so much.

According to his parents, Robbie's behavior had turned hostile and he often threatened to run away. He had become violent and disagreeable, which was so unlike his previous personality that they found it hard to belief that these changes could be dismissed as nothing more than the onset of his teenage years. Robbie's nature had changed so dramatically that it was almost as if a separate personality had overcome his own. Comments like this put Father Bishop on alert. Robbie's parents knew nothing of possession and yet what they were describing was a textbook example of the early stages of the phenomenon. He was disturbed by what they told him but he tried not to show it.

After talking with Robbie, Father Bishop went from room to room of the Roanoke Drive house and blessed each of them, offering soft prayers in Latin and gesturing the sign of the cross with his right hand. He also sprinkled holy water about as he gave his blessing. He spent extra time in the bedroom that

Robbie was using, giving a "special blessing" that he repeated over Robbie's bed. This ritual was the "priestly blessing" that Father Reinert had advised Bishop to give. It was a sort of "low level" exorcism against what the Jesuits called "infestation," the mildest form of diabolical activity. The strange happenings that Robbie's family reported -- from the scratchings in the walls to the shaking bed -- seemed to indicate that entities were manifesting around Robbie. These spirits could often be countered by this mild sort of exorcism, which was carried out to cleanse a place rather than a person.

Even while carrying out this Christian tradition, Bishop would have suspected that this type of exorcism would be in vain. Robbie was plagued no matter where he went and blessing the house would have made no difference. It was likely that the situation had already progressed beyond the point of infestation and on to the next stage, known as obsession. In that stage, according to a Catholic treatise written in 1906, the demon never forces the victim to lose consciousness but torments him in such a manner that the demon's action is manifest. The scratching and thumping in Robbie's house in Maryland, would have been signs of the infestation stage. The scratches on Robbie's body, which Bishop had heard about but had not yet seen himself, indicated obsession. What had not yet appeared were signs of the third stage -- possession.

Bishop also brought a relic with him to the home, which he attached to Robbie's pillow with a safety pin. It was a cloth pouch that contained a small bit of material in a glass case. The material was a tiny fragment that was a second-class relic of St. Margaret Mary. A second-class relic is a piece of something that was touched by the saint, like clothing or wood. A first-class relic would be a chip of bone of a lock of hair from the saint's body. Jesuits were especially devoted to St. Margaret Mary Alacoque, a seventeenth century French nun, because her spiritual advisor was a Jesuit. He encouraged her when, against initial opposition from the Church, she began what became worldwide devotion to the Sacred Heart of Jesus. By attaching this relic to Robbie's pillow, Father Bishop was asking for the intercession of a woman who claimed to have had a mystical encounter with Jesus. She said that Jesus had appeared before her, placed her heart inside of his own and then drew it out, "like a burning heart-shaped flame." Catholic immigrants brought the practice of revering the Sacred Heart to America. Countless homes and churches across the country have images hanging inside of them with Jesus revealing his flaming, bleeding heart.

When it was time for Robbie to go to bed for the night, he went upstairs to the room that Bishop had blessed. A few minutes later, Father Bishop went into his room and told him good night. They talked for a few minutes and then Bishop left with Robbie chuckling over some small joke. He went back downstairs and was preparing to leave when all of them heard something upstairs. They listened

71

for a moment and then were stunned by the sounds of thumping and banging on the second floor. When Robbie began screaming, all of them ran for the stairs.

Father Bishop was shocked by what he saw when he entered the door of Robbie's bedroom. According to the "exorcist's diary":

Even after the blessing of the house and in spite of the relic, the swaying was evident and the scratches appeared.... When Father Bishop sprinkled St. Ignatius holy water on the bed in the form of a cross, the movement ceased quite abruptly but began again when Father stepped out of the room. During the course of the 15 minutes of activity a sharp pain seemed to have struck Roland on his stomach and he cried out. The mother quickly pulled back the bed covers and lifted the boy's pajama top enough to show zigzag scratches in bold red lines on the boy's abdomen.

Bishop added that Robbie was "perfectly still" on the bed and that he did not exert any physical effort. Regardless, the mattress on the bed jerked back and forth and thumped up and down without any logical explanation. Moments after the holy water was sprinkled onto the bed, as stated in the diary, the movement stopped and then started back up again when Father Bishop left the room.

It was at that moment that Robbie cried out and his mother lifted his pajama top to show the bold red lines that had appeared on his stomach. According to Bishop, Robbie had been in clear view of at least six witnesses during this entire time and no one had seen him create the scratches himself and had seen no movement that could have caused the marks to appear.

The mattress continued to shake in spurts of movement until about 11:15 p.m. and then it stopped moving as suddenly as it had started. Robbie was at peace for the rest of the evening and his relatives later said that it was the most peaceful night since Robbie and his parents had come to St. Louis.

The next day, Thursday, March 10, Bishop took his concerns about the case to one of his closest friends, Father William S. Bowdern, S.J. He told him about what he had heard and seen at the house on Roanoke Drive and Bowdern listened intently. Bowdern was not on the faculty of St. Louis University and unlike most Jesuits, he was not a teacher. In 1949, he was the pastor of St. Francis Xavier Church, located at the corner of Grand and Lindell.

Although the church had been built to serve students and faculty at the university, it was also a parish church that served a large Catholic community near the university. As the pastor, Bowdern answered to the rector of the school and Archbishop Ritter, who was in charge of all of the priests in the archdiocese. However, he also had a lot of freedom. Although a member of the Jesuit community, he was not part of the university faculty, and he belonged more to his parishioners than to the Jesuits. He also lived apart from the Jesuits at the university, in a rectory, just as any church pastor would do. Bowdern was the administrator of a busy church at that time, with a full schedule of baptisms, weddings, funerals and wakes. He had new Jesuit priests who served as his assistants but Bowdern carried most of the load. He had many years experience dealing with people and their problems and he listened carefully to the story that Bishop told him.

In 1949, Bowdern was fifty-two years old and a native of St. Louis. He had joined the Society of Jesus when he was seventeen, after completing high school at the St. Louis University's school. He was short and stocky with black hair and a square jaw and had a reputation for keeping his nerve. After his ordination, he had been made principal of the high school at St. Mary's College in Kansas, where he had also been a teacher during his years of Jesuit study. He moved on to St. Louis University High School, where he also became principal, and then was appointed rector of Campion Jesuit High in Prairie du Chien, Wisconsin. In 1942, he began a four year stint as a U.S. Army Chaplain, serving in war-torn Europe and on the battlefields of China, Burma and India. He left the Army in 1946 and became pastor of the St. Francis Xavier Church. His no-nonsense approach as a priest who had seen the horror of war, as well as his compassionate nature, must have appealed to Bishop and caused him to seek out Bowdern about Robbie's case. He needed the advice of his friend and he also needed counsel from a man who was often described as being "totally fearless."

Father Bishop never reported on his initial meeting with Father Bowdern about the case but many feel that he saw himself as a simple, pious man who was drawn into something that was beyond his knowledge and experience. With that in mind, he brought the case to Father Bowdern, who was a pastor and Army chaplain. It also may have been because Bishop considered Bowdern to be a holy man one of the criteria needed for an exorcist . To Jesuits, there is a distinction between being pious and being holy. Piety can be seen and acted out while holiness is internal and soulful.

Some would say that Bishop was the more pious of the two men. In the case of Robbie Doe, he had acted, with his second-class relic and holy water, in a pious way. Piety, to many, including Jesuits, was often seen as an overabundance of faith. There are those who believe a less pious Jesuit would have asked more questions, would have investigated the family background and would have waited longer before taking the situation into the realm of the mysterious with holy water and articles of faith. But those who would say such things were not in Bishop's position. He had witnessed something that, to him, was beyond reason. He saw the mattress shake and saw the marks appear on Robbie's body. He did

73

start to ask questions and investigate the background of the case but his first instinct had been to react in a pious manner. As a result, he had taken the case from strange to beyond the unknown in a short amount of time.

Befuddled by his first encounter with Robbie's case, Bishop may not have wanted to rely on his piety to figure out what was going on. He may have wanted help from a witness that he knew he could trust. He had the perfect person in his friend William Bowdern, a seasoned man and a Jesuit priest that even other Jesuits referred to as a holy man.

While Father Bishop was conferring with his friend in the case, Robbie and family were continuing to deal with the bizarre manifestations at the Roanoke Drive house. That Thursday passed uneventfully but when Robbie went to bed that night, the noises started again. The sound of scratching filled his bedroom and thumping sounds, like those made by stomping feet, could be heard throughout the house. A little later, the mattress began to shake and bump again and the relic of St. Margaret Mary was thrown across the room. Robbie swore that he had never touched it. The clasp on the safety pin, he claimed and his mother agreed, apparently opened by itself and came off the pillow.

On Friday, Robbie's cousin stopped in at Father Bishop's office and told him about what had occurred the night before. He told her that he would arrange to return to the house that night and would bring Father Bowdern with him. Robbie's uncle picked up both men at the St. Francis Xavier Church that evening, just after 10:00 p.m.

The visit had to be planned so late in the evening because Father Bowdern was extremely busy with an exhaustive novena that consisted of nine days of special devotions at the church, leaving him nearly exhausted. Each day there had been prayer services at noon, in the afternoon, at the dinner hour and then again at 9:00 p.m. Bowdern officiated during all of them, giving a homily at each service. The major service, complete with a choir, was held at 9:00 that Friday night. The church was packed for the end of the novena, which was in honor of the church's patron saint, Francis Xavier.

When the two priests left the church that night, Bowdern brought with him two of the parish's most valuable relics, one of which was a first-class relic of St. Francis Xavier. The saint had been a missionary in India and Japan and had died in 1552 on an island off the coast of China and was buried there. Two months later, his grave was opened and accounts of the time state that his body had not decayed. The body was then taken to India and enshrined in a church. The Jesuit Superior General ordered the right arm of the corpse to be severed at the elbow and brought to Rome, where it was placed in the altar of a church.

The relic that Father Bowdern brought to the house on Roanoke Drive was a piece of the bone from Xavier's right arm. It rested in a glass container that was lined with velvet and then placed in a gold reliquary. He also brought along a crucifix that had been hollowed out to house two other first-class relics. One was that of St. Peter Canisius, a Jesuit theologian, writer and preacher from the sixteenth century, and the other a collective relic from a group of saints known as the North American martyrs, six Jesuits and two lay assistants who were killed by Indians during the seventeenth century.

The two priests arrived at the house around 10:30 p.m. and Bishop introduced Bowdern, who told Robbie's family that he planned to offer a priestly blessing. His real agenda, however, was to sit down and talk with Robbie and see what he could learn from the boy. He had many years of experience dealing with boys around Robbie's age, thanks to his positions at high schools and as the pastor of the church. He chatted with the young man for a half hour or so and asked him a number of questions about what had been taking place. He never appeared judgmental and avoided expressing any real opinions or ideas about what was occurring. Bowdern thanked Robbie and shook hands with him in an adult manner and then his mother sent the boy upstairs to get ready for bed. His mother and father tucked him in just a little after 11:00 p.m. but a few minutes later, he was already crying for help.

The priests, Robbie's parents, his cousin and her parents all ran up the stairs to the room where Robbie could be heard calling out. When they crowded into the room, they found him sitting up, his face white. On other nights when strange events had occurred, Robbie had seemed almost in a trance, unaware of what was going on around him. On this night, though, he seemed like a scared little boy. He had felt some sort of force in the room, he told the adults. The pin on the relic of St. Margaret Mary had opened again and had once more sailed across the room. It struck a mirror with a solid snap but the glass didn't break.

Robbie held up his arm for them to look at and they all noticed the appearance of two scratches on his outer forearm that made the sign of a cross. Father Bishop examined the marks and later wrote that Robbie told him the pain from the scratches "was similar to that produced by the scratch of a thorn. The cross remained evident for approximately 45 minutes."

Father Bowdern, although likely a little surprised by what he had seen, calmly dealt with the situation in the way that he knew best. He quietly read the novena prayer of St. Francis Xavier and then blessed Robbie by moving the Xavier relic over him in the sign of the cross. Bowdern then pinned the crucifix reliquary that he had brought with him to Robbie's pillow, right next to the relic of St. Margaret Mary. This time, there was no shaking of the bed or weird scratching noises.

Robbie seemed at peace now and so everyone wished him a good night and returned to the downstairs living room. It was at this point that Father Bishop began collecting the facts of the case from everyone who was present. He labeled his file "Case Study" and began the initial notes that would become the "exorcist's diary" that has been mentioned so often within these pages. The heading of the file read:

Roland Doe
Son of Mr. and Mrs. Edwin Doe, Middle Class Washington Suburban Development
Birth: June 1, 1935; Religion: Evangelical Lutheran, baptized six months after birth by Lutheran minister
Maternal Grandmother ---- practicing Catholic until the age of fourteen years
Father ---- baptized Catholic, but no instruction or practice
Mother ---- baptized Lutheran
Roland and his mother visited in St. Louis at Bel Nor, Normandy, at the home of Mr. and Mrs. L.C. Doe

Father Bishop did most of the questioning as he detailed the background of the case. Occasionally, Father Bowdern chimed in with a question or two. Bishop wrote down everything Robbie's parents told him, writing down events that dated all of the way back to the beginning of the case in January. After filling a number of pages with notes, the two priests prepared to leave. Before they could, though, the entire group heard a crashing sound coming from upstairs.

They rushed back up the steps to Robbie's room. The boy explained that he had been dozing when a bottle of holy water, left by Father Bishop on Wednesday, flew off the table next to Robbie's bed. It soared across the room and landed hard on the wooden floor but didn't break.

Without saying a word, Father Bowdern removed a rosary from his pocket and draped it around Robbie's neck. He stood on one side of the bed and motioned Father Bishop to the other side. Together, they began to recite the rosary and when they were finished with the prayers, Bowdern sat down and began to tell Robbie about three children, about Robbie's age, who had a remarkable experience at Fatima in Portugal in 1917. His soft voice soothed the boy, relaying the story of how the young people had seen a vision of a beautiful woman, the mother of Jesus and the "Mary" in the "Hail Mary" prayers the priests had just recited. Prayers that were offered up to Mary, Father Bowdern explained, reached Jesus and he responded to the prayers.

76

The simple story seemed to calm Robbie down and he sleepily wished Father Bowdern and his silent audience good night. Bowdern and Bishop both blessed the boy one last time and then at nearly 1:00 a.m., Robbie's uncle drove them back to the campus. The strange night finally seemed to be over.

As it turned out, though, the night at the house on Roanoke Drive was just getting started. A few minutes after Robbie's uncle left to drive the priests back to St. Louis University, the remaining adults heard the sound of something heavy scraping across the floor of Robbie's bedroom. They hurriedly climbed the staircase once more and turned the knob to open the bedroom door. The knob twisted but the door immediately banged into something directly on the other side. Robbie's father put his shoulder to the door and heaved against the wooden panel. It slowly edged open and he was startled to find that the door had been blocked by a heavy bookcase. It had been slammed up against the door, having somehow dragged itself from the far side of the room. Robbie's father was barely able to move it out of the way to gain access to the room. He believed that it was unlikely, if not impossible, that Robbie could have moved the bookcase himself as some sort of prank. Robbie did not appear to have left the bed. He was sitting up, startled by their entrance, and he looked dazed and confused about what was occurring. The first thing his mother noticed about the room was that a stool that had been next to the head of the bed was now turned upside down at the foot of it.

She pushed her way into the room and lay down next to her son, hoping to comfort him. His aunt and cousin wrestled the bookcase back to its place along the wall and put the stool back where it belonged. Finally, a few minutes later, everyone left but Robbie's mother. Exhausted and scared, she laid down next to her son and held the boy until he fell asleep. But sleep would not come for the anxious parent.

She lay there in the dark for some time and then suddenly was aware of some sort of "force" in the room with them. The stool that was sitting next to the bed fell over with a loud crack. The noise awakened Robbie and he later said that he felt something moving underneath his pillow -- the crucifix that Father Bowdern had pinned there had come undone and was slithering under the bed sheets. In a panic, Robbie reached for the St. Margaret Mary relic and while the safety pin was still there and in place, the relic had vanished. Moments later, the shaking and the scratching of the mattress began. It quivered only slightly at first and then became more violent. The scratching became louder and louder and the mattress began to slam up and down against the bed frame, creating a terrifying and chaotic racket.

Robbie's mother sprang out of bed and took her son with her. They fled from the room, just as the others were coming up the stairs to see what all of the noise

77

was. They could hear the banging, thudding and scratching from downstairs and were not surprised to see Robbie and his mother flying down the steps.

The entire family spent the remainder of the night wrapped in blankets on the floor and furniture of the living room. What was happening to Robbie? No one knew that the nightmare, as bad as it already seemed, was only beginning.

On Saturday afternoon, Robbie's cousin visited Father Bishop's office and told him of the things that she had seen and heard the night before. She sat down with him for a time and expressed her worries about what was happening. Bishop promised her that he would not let the situation rest and now that Father Bowdern had completed the novena at his church, he would be able to devote more time to the situation as well. The two men already realized that demonic possession was a grim reality that they might have to face. However, before they reached that point, there was much in the way of investigation and research that had to be done.

It cannot be denied that all of the incidents that had occurred in St. Louis, including the moving of the wooden bookcase, could have been caused by Robbie. Of course, just because he could have accomplished these happenings, did not mean that he did -- simply that he *could* have. Robbie *could* have been perpetrating an elaborate hoax or he could have been mentally ill, perhaps even on the verge of a nervous breakdown. The *Rituale Romanum* warned a prospective exorcist that he "should not believe too readily that a person is possessed by an evil spirit" for he could be disturbed instead.

Did Robbie really meet the conditions for being possessed? There are many who believe that Robbie's case, chronicled by his family and carefully recorded by Bishop, showed a steady progression toward diabolical possession. The case began with the infestation in Maryland, the strange poltergeist activity that revolved around the boy, and then went on to obsession, when Robbie began to be scratched and marked. After that, following the prescribed sequence of events, would be full-fledged possession. Did Bishop and Bowdern believe they could stop the progression before things got worse?

We will never know because unfortunately, there is no reliable, clear-cut information about how the decision was reached by Bowdern and Bishop to request an exorcism for Robbie. According to church doctrine, there are a number of different conditions that have to be met to show that someone is truly possessed, including speaking in foreign tongues and revealing information that he would have no way of knowing. Whether or not these conditions were met is not for me to say or judge but regardless, Bowdern and Bishop went to Archbishop Joseph E. Ritter for permission to perform an exorcism on March 14.

78

The Jesuits had no idea how Ritter would respond to the request. Surprisingly, he promptly agreed.

And the exorcism began...

PART 3: EXORCISM

One night, the boy brushed off his handlers and soared through the air at Father Bowdern standing at some distance from his bed with the ritual book in his hands. Presumably, the Father was about to be attacked but the boy got no further than the book. And when his hands hit that ---- I assure you, Gene, I saw it with my own eyes ---- he didn't tear the book, he dissolved it! The book vaporized into confetti and fell in fine small pieces all over the floor.
Father Charles O'Hara --- witness to the 1949 Exorcism

Interestingly, despite their compassion for the boy and his family, neither Father Bishop nor Father Bowdern wanted to act as Robbie's exorcist. Thanks to the research they had conducted over the weekend of March 12 and 13, they found enough in the literature of possession to convince them that they were not qualified for the job. While the practice of exorcism was included in the teachings of the Church, by 1949, it was a very rare occurrence. Possession was no longer, as it had once been, a matter of ordinary experience. During the Middle Ages, possession was so common in Europe that the Church needed an abundance of exorcists but in the modern times of the twentieth century they had become a vestige of a time long past.

Although no record has ever been made public as to what correspondence or discussion took place between the Jesuit community and Archbishop Ritter about Robbie's case, what is known is that Bowdern received the permission of his superior to write a letter to Ritter, asking that an exorcism be authorized and an exorcist be chosen. Bowdern asked that he not be chosen for the task because he did not feel that he was a man who could be described as "holy," as an exorcist was required to be. He did offer to present the case to the archbishop, though, and gave a brief description of the events that had been plaguing Robbie and his family.

Meanwhile, as the Jesuit's research was going on, the family reported that the eerie happenings were continuing in the house. Objects were moving around Robbie's room at night, the mattress shook and trembled and the relic of St. Margaret Mary had developed a habit of disappearing and then re-appearing again in various places.

After Bowdern submitted his report, he began thinking about recruiting an exorcist for Robbie. He anticipated an authorization from Archbishop Ritter and knew that a man would have to be found. He believed the person should be a theologian and preferably a Jesuit, so he began making inquiries in the community. Two men were actually asked but both of them politely refused Bowdern's request. It would later be stated that the two men who declined were not skeptical of the case but simply felt they did not have the strength to carry out an exorcism.

Archbishop Ritter received the request and report on March 14 and immediately began researching the information, unsure of what to do about it. Earlier in the book, it was mentioned that Father Reinert was concerned about the way that an exorcism might appear to the public in regards to St. Louis University. It was a delicate time for the school but it was an even more delicate time for the archdiocese. The backlash that might come from publicity about the exorcism could set the Church back decades if not a century or two and could make Ritter look foolish among his peers, who saw him as a leader who could take the Catholic Church into a new era.

Joseph Ritter was fifty-four years old when he became the Archbishop of St. Louis and had already gained such a reputation at his previous post in Indianapolis that Pope Pius XII never questioned his decision a year later when he followed the Jesuit lead in the city and desegregated the archdiocese. When a number of die-hard Catholic segregationists threatened to defy him, Ritter announced that he would excommunicate anyone who stood in the way of opening the churches and schools to people of color. The surprised opponents quickly backed down and the changes went smoothly, just as they had at St. Louis University a few years before. This approach to moral issues served him well and made him a well-known American churchman. He would become a cardinal in 1961 and at the Vatican II council in 1962, he would lead the progressive faction, which included a number of Jesuits.

It's likely that Ritter did not like what was brought to him by Father Bowdern. He would not have been comfortable exposing the archdiocese to

81

ridicule and also likely knew that many other bishops and archbishops in the United States had rejected requests for exorcism, forcing the alleged victims to move to another diocese or simply to end up in a mental hospital. Ritter could have done this as well but he had a reputation for solving the problems that were brought to him. Hours of thought and worry must have gone into his decision but eventually, he chose to authorize the exorcism.

Once he made this decision, he also had to choose a priest to carry out the ritual. He knew the criteria needed for an effective exorcist and likely knew many priests who could qualify for the job and many others who could not. According to the *Rituale Romanum*, an exorcist "must be properly distinguished for his piety, his prudence and integrity of life. He should fulfill this devout undertaking in all constancy and humility, being utterly immune to any striving for human aggrandizement, and relying, not on his own but on divine power. Moreover, he ought to be of mature years, and revered not alone for his office but for his moral qualities." With this in mind, he could reach out to the faculty at any seminary, Jesuit or otherwise, request an exorcist from another archdiocese or even select a priest from his own chancery. After some thought, Ritter chose Father Bowdern.

Ritter never made it clear as to why he chose Bowdern for the task but probably figured that he was as qualified as anyone else in the archdiocese and as we will soon see, Ritter wanted the exorcism to be a private issue and that he knew the case better than anyone else. His only order to Father Bowdern was to promise never to discuss the exorcism with anyone. Bowdern readily agreed but as the reader will discover in the pages to follow, he was only of the only people aside from Robbie and his family involved in the exorcism who did not talk about in years to come.

Bowdern would never discuss the case but he decided on his own that Father Bishop should continue the report that he was compiling on the case as an account of what happened each day and night. This report became the "exorcist's diary" that has been referred to many times already. Bowdern's reasoning was that since it was difficult to find authentic, current literature on cases of possession, the diary would be "most helpful to anyone placed in a similar position as an exorcist in any future case."

The exorcism of Robbie Doe officially began in the afternoon of Wednesday, March 16 but the chronology of the case is extremely confusing. It is not always clear how long Robbie stayed at the house on Roanoke Drive but it is known that he was taken to the Alexian Brothers Hospital in south St. Louis, possibly for as long as a month, and that portions of the exorcism were also carried out in the rectory of the St. Francis Xavier Church. The rectory has since been demolished and replaced. Stories have circulated from students who once attended St. Louis

University that strange sounds were often heard coming from the rectory during the period when Robbie was there and noxious odors were experienced wafting from the windows. The attention that this brought to the rectory may have been part of the decision to move Robbie to the Alexian Brothers Hospital. This may simply be part of the folklore that currently surrounds the case but no one, at this point, can say for sure.

It also isn't certain how many people were actually actively involved in the exorcism. The names of the exorcists given out in St. Louis were Father Bowdern, Father Bishop and Father Lawrence Kenny. Father Charles O'Hara of Marquette University in Milwaukee was also present as a witness, as was Father William Van Roo, and there were undoubtedly several hospital staff members and seminary students who were also in attendance.

One of these students was Walter Halloran. In 1949, he was a strapping young former football player who had been asked to help with the exorcism by holding Robbie down. Exorcisms were known for being often violent rituals and the Jesuits must have felt that the young man would prove to be very useful. For some reason, though, Halloran was removed from the exorcism about one week before it came to end, leaving his accounts of it rather incomplete. In spite of this, he became an essential source of information about the case, not only to author Thomas Allen but to journalists and other authors, like myself. I spoke with Father Halloran a couple of months before his death and he provided me with much of the information about the exorcism as it appears in the book.

Halloran would have uncertain and often conflicting recollections about the case but many hospital staff members would remember the events with fear. Steve Erdmann, who wrote about the case in 1975, personally knew at least one of the nurses involved. The nurse's name was Ernest Schaffer and he was barely able to talk about the case more than two decades after it happened. He stated that the priests had a "terrible time" during Robbie's hospital stay. He had many conversations with the priests and believed that what he saw was supernatural in origin. He said that he cleaned vomit out of the boy's room on several different occasions.

Something very strange happened in St. Louis in 1949 -- but what was it?

On the afternoon of March 16, Father Bowdern sent a message to Walter Halloran. Halloran was a twenty-six-year-old man who was studying at St. Louis University. He had been a Jesuit for eight years and had known Bowdern since he had attended Campion Jesuit High, where Bowdern had been rector. The older man had been one of Halloran's inspirations for becoming a Jesuit and he had great respect for him. Thanks to their long relationship, the two men had developed a good friendship, despite the fact that they were so different in age.

83

 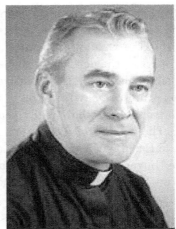

Left Father William Bowdern and Right Father Walter Halloran, who was a Jesuit student at the time of the exorcism. As the youngest man involved, he would live to pass on many first-hand accounts of what occurred.

The message that Halloran received that afternoon was a request that he drive Father Bowdern on an errand that evening. Bowdern never drove and Halloran often took him on parish errands and on sick calls, so he readily agreed. He brought the parish car around to the rectory about 9:00 p.m. and found both Father Bowdern and Father Bishop waiting for him. Father Bowdern gave him an address and after checking the map, Halloran drove to the northwest side, searching for Roanoke Drive. The two priests spoke in quiet conversation, which Halloran paid little attention to, but he did notice that they were both wearing cassocks and carrying surplices.

When they reached the house, Bowdern invited the young man to come inside with them. Years later, he admitted that he was surprised by the invitation but even more surprised by what Bowdern said next. The Jesuit explained, "I'll be doing an exorcism. I want you to hold the boy down in case it's needed."

Knowing there was no time to ask questions, Halloran followed Bowdern and Bishop up the front steps and they all went inside. Bowdern introduced Halloran to Robbie and his family and then he sat down with the boy and explained to him that he was going to bring him a new kind of help. Bowdern explained that there were "special prayers" for situations like this. He also told them all that he thought it was time to get them started.

Robbie told everyone good night and then went upstairs and got ready for bed. His mother waited for a few minutes and then went up to the boy's bedroom.

A short time after, she stepped to the top of the stairwell and called down to them that Robbie was in bed.

Father Bowdern went upstairs alone and spent a short time with Robbie. Bishop later reported that he had helped Robbie to examine his conscience and to make an act of contrition. There is no way to know what the two of them talked about but if there had been a confession of a hoax or anything that would have caused Bowdern to doubt the authenticity of what was taking place, then he would have undoubtedly called off the exorcism. Instead, he came downstairs and asked Father Bishop and Walter Halloran to come upstairs with him. Before going back up the stairs, the two priests prepared themselves by unrolling their purple stoles from their pockets, kissing them and then placing them around their necks. They each carried a copy of the *Rituale Romanum* and Bowdern had a bottle of holy water as well.

A few moments later, they nervously started upstairs to begin the ritual. They all knew that an exorcism could be a dire spiritual and physical struggle as the demon that takes control of the person also tries to break the faith and physical wellness of the exorcist. Prior to coming to the house on Roanoke Drive, Father Bowdern had said Mass, had made his general confession to Father Kenny and had spent much of the day in prayer. He had also started to fast, which was recommended in the *Rituale Romanum*. He would continue to do so over the course of the exhausting weeks to follow and it was said that from the time he first learned of Robbie's plight until the exorcism had run its course, Bowdern lost nearly forty pounds.

The priests, along with Walter Halloran, walked into the bedroom with Father Bowdern leading the way. They were followed a few moments later by Robbie's mother and his aunt and uncle. Father Bowdern crossed the room to the opposite side of the bed and made the sign of a cross as he sprinkled the bed and the boy with holy water. Then, he knelt down on the floor and Father Bishop also knelt on the other side of the bed. The family members also knelt down, leaving Halloran unsure of what to do. After a moment's hesitation, Father Bishop motioned for him to kneel as well. He lowered himself at the foot of the bed.

Father Bowdern led the group in a series of prayers of faith, hope, love and contrition. Robbie, who was lying in bed, joined in as best that he could. The priest then began what was called the Litany of the Saints, asking the Lord to have mercy on them. The prayer asked for Holy Mary to pray for them, uttering in Latin what were familiar words to the Jesuits.

As the words spilled forth, the mattress on the bed reportedly began to move. According to Walter Halloran, he saw it start to go up and down before his eyes. It levitated several inches, banged back down, lifted again and then settled with a thud. Halloran looked over at Father Bishop, his eyes wide with surprise.

"It's no problem, Walt," Father Bishop whispered to the young man. "Just go ahead and pray."

Father Bishop resumed the Litany, which summoned aid for Robbie from the saints, including the angels, the holy innocents and virgins, the martyrs, priests, monks and founders of religious orders. Then it shifted from the names of the saints to pleas to God ---- "O Lord, Deliver us." As the prayers continued, Father Bowdern continued to recite phrases in Latin, which were answered by Father Bishop. As they continued, the mattress on the bed continued to shake and jump up and down, as if keeping time with the words. Finally, the prayers turned to a recital of words from the Book of Psalms.

Soon, the words of the actual exorcism were spoken and what happened next was passed along by Walter Halloran. They were events that he still remembered more than fifty years later. As Father Bishop began to loudly speak the next words, Robbie literally screamed.

"I command thee, unclean spirit, whosoever thou art, along with all thine associates who have taken possession of this servant of God that, by the mysteries of the Incarnation, Passion, Resurrection and Ascension of our Lord Jesus Christ by the descent of the Holy Spirit, by the coming of our Lord, unto judgment, thou shalt tell me some sign or other thy name and the day and hour of thy departure. I command thee, moreover, to obey me to the letter, I who though unworthy, am a minister of God....."

Those gathered in the room quickly realized that Robbie's screams were not cries of fear, but of pain. The boy threw back the covers from the bed and he tore open his pajama top. Across his stomach were three long, red welts. He screamed again and again. Each time that Father Bowdern stated the word *Dominus* Lord or *Deus* God , new welts and scratches appeared. His mother later recalled that it seemed as though something inside of Robbie was trying to claw its way out. The lines continued to appear, creating long, bloody slices across his body. Father Bishop later described the scratches as "marks raised up above the surface of the skin, similar to an engraving" and noted that little lines of glistening blood appeared on his legs, thighs, stomach and back. Scratches also marked his throat and face, even though his hands were in plain sight to everyone gathered in the room. There was no way that Robbie could have physically made the marks on his own body.

While this was occurring, Father Bowdern never looked up from the *Rituale Romanum*. He continued to recite the prayers of exorcism and when he completed it, he started over again. As he started to read it, something twitched on Robbie's leg. Bowdern demanded again that the demon identify itself and red

86

welts formed on the boy's skin. It was, the witnesses later said, an image "like the Devil." It had arms that seemed to be webbed, "giving the hideous appearance of a bat."

Father Bowdern continued to read from the prayer book and at the next mention of God's name *Deus* , letters suddenly appeared on Robbie's narrow chest. The scratches looked and felt to the touch like scratches made by a cat. They spelled out a jagged word that looked like "hell." The word had been scratched so that they faced Robbie and he began to weep when he looked down at the letters. The letters bled so much that Father Bishop dabbed at the scratches with a handkerchief that came away stained with red.

Father Bowdern read the next passage, again demanding that the demon offer a sign as to when it would depart from the boy and more letters appeared on Robbie's skin. Bloody scratches marred his stomach, spelling out "go," and then another red mark appeared on his leg, looking like a crooked letter "X." Bishop wondered if this meant that the demon planned to leave in 10 days. He hoped that it did but this would, of course, turn out to be a false assumption.

Soon after the dark "X" appeared, Robbie seemed to simply collapse and he fell into a deep sleep. Father Bishop looked the boy over and began to count the marks that had appeared on him. He lost count after noting more than two dozen because many of them were clustered into patches of welts.

While this was going on, Father Bowdern continued to read from the *Rituale* and to recite prayers of exorcism and pleas for assistance from St. Michael the Archangel and others.

As the words of the prayer left the priest's lips, Robbie began to stir in his sleep. He turned and twisted back and forth with his eyes tightly closed. He mumbled words under his breath and thrashed up and down, punching the wooden headboard of the bed and tearing at his pillow. He seemed unaware of what he was doing as he convulsed in his sleep, turning violent and angry.

Father Bowdern leaned over the boy and sprinkled his shaking body with holy water. Suddenly, Robbie awakened with a jolt. He told the priests that he dreamed that he had been fighting with a huge "red devil." The creature was trying to keep the boy from escaping from a burning pit where Robbie had been imprisoned. There was a set of iron gates at the top of the pit, the boy told them, and he knew that he had to go through them to get away. He told them that he felt that he was beating the devil and might be able to escape.

The two priests exchanged glances. Although Robbie could not have understood the Latin words of the prayer to St. Michael, the boy had somehow comprehended the message of them in his dream. Was Robbie cleverly telling the Jesuits what they wanted to hear? Or was the supernatural somehow at work?

Having already dismissed the idea that Robbie could be perpetrating a hoax, Father Bowdern decided to continue the exorcism, beginning again with the most powerful prayer:

I cast thee out, thou unclean spirit, along with the least encroachment of the wicked enemy, and every phantom and diabolical legion. In the name of our Lord Jesus Christ, depart and vanish from this creature of God....

According to the accounts of Walter Halloran and Father Bishop, Robbie lapsed back into the restless unconsciousness from earlier. His eyes moved rapidly back and forth beneath his eyelids as Father Bowdern made the sign of a cross over him. His arms twitched outward, waving wildly in the air. Halloran grabbed for the boys hand's, trying to keep him from hitting one of the priests.

Father Bowdern continued to read as Robbie rolled back and forth:

For it is He who commands thee, He who ordered thee cast down from the heights of heaven into the nethermost pit of the earth. He it is who commands thee, who once ordered the sea and wind and the storm to obey. Hence, pay heed, Satan, and tremble, thou enemy of the faith, thou foe of the human race! For thou are the carrier of death and the robber of life. Thou art the shirker of justice and the root of all evil, the fomenter or vice, the seducer of men, the traitor of the nations, the instigator of envy, the font of avarice, the course of discord, the exciter of sorrows....

Robbie began to thrash even more violently and Walter Halloran came around the bed and tried to hold the boy down. Years later, Halloran would speak often about his attempts to restrain the boy and he told of being punched by him several times and at one point, having his nose broken. He joked that Robbie "was no Mike Tyson" but he also admitted that, even as a well-conditioned athlete, he was often unable to restrain the thin, ninety-five-pound boy. On this night, as Robbie continually jerked away from the young man, Robbie's uncle stepped in to help. He grabbed one of his Robbie's shoulders and Halloran held the other. The boy shouted at them, demanding that they let him go, but the men held firm.

Father Bowdern continued to pray and he moved his thumb over Robbie's brow, tracing the sign of the cross three times in the name of God the Father, God the Son and God the Holy Spirit. Robbie continued to struggle as the exorcism went on.

Father Bowdern read: "Make way for God the Holy Spirit through this sign of the Holy Cross of our Lord Jesus Christ. Who liveth and reigneth with the Father and the selfsame Holy Spirit, God, forever and ever."

88

Father Bishop responded in a whispered voice: "Amen."

Bowdern: "O Lord, hear my prayer."

Bishop: "And let my cry come unto Thee."

Bowdern: "The Lord be with you."

Bishop: "And with they spirit."

Father Bowdern took another deep breath and in a hoarse voice, continued to read. As the prayers continued, he glanced at Robbie, who flailed about and struck at the two men holding him. With his eyes shut, he turned his head and spat, with uncanny accuracy, into the faces of Walter Halloran and his uncle. With an animal-like cry, he worked one of his arms free and lashed out at his uncle. The man was struck across the face but he still managed to force Robbie's arm back down onto the bed.

The prayers continued and Father Bowdern traced the sign of the cross on Robbie's head. The boy jolted forward and, again with his eyes closed, spit and struck the priest in the face. Father Bowdern remained outwardly unaffected. He simply raised a hand as a shield and continued to read from the prayer book. He made three crosses over the "hell" that had appeared on Robbie's chest and endured more spitting and several swift kicks from the boy's jerking legs. He continued to read the prayers, making slashing crosses in the air at the appropriate times. His hand moved in vicious cuts, mirroring the violence that was occurring on the bed.

On sweat-soaked sheets, Robbie writhed and grimaced in his trance, shaking, twisting and spitting. He continued to fight against his assailants, as strong now as he had been hours before, when the exorcism had started. Halloran and Robbie's uncle continued to fight with the boy but they were exhausted and their grips were weakening. The faces of both men were red with strain and their shirts were wet with their own sweat. Robbie's mother and aunt huddled together at the foot of the bed, gaping at the scene with both terror and grief. Father Bishop was also near to collapse. His hair was damp with sweat and his surplice was stained by the blood and spit that Robbie had expelled at him.

Father Bowdern looked at the people around him, knowing that everyone was tired and frightened. He also knew that the ritual had to continue. He held the ritual book in his left hand and with his right, he poured a bottle of holy water onto Robbie's head. The boy awoke, startled and then he sat up for a moment before falling back onto the damp pillow. He was now strangely calm and he quietly asked for a glass of water, which his mother went to get from a bathroom down the hall. By the time she had returned, Robbie was asleep again - and once again fighting and struggling with his uncle and Walter Halloran.

Several times during the night, as prayers came to an end, Father Bowdern repeated the process of pouring holy water on Robbie's face. The Jesuits both felt that he was much calmer when he was awake and when the water did not rouse him, Father Bishop would lightly slap his face until he awoke.

Finally, hours after the ritual had begun, came the last prayer of exorcism. Father Bowdern began to read, making crosses in the air above Robbie's flailing body:

I cast thee out, every unclean spirit, every phantom, every encroachment of Satan, in the name of Jesus Christ of Nazareth, who after John baptized him, was led into the desert and vanquished thee in thy citadel. Cease thy attack on man, whom He had made for His honor and glory out of the slime of the earth. Tremble before wretched man, not in the condition of human frailty but in the likeness of the mighty God....

Father Bowdern continued the final prayer, his voice raised to the point that he was nearly shouting. Even with his harsh cries, though, he could sometimes only barely be heard about the grunts, yells and guttural barks that Robbie was making as he rolled back and forth on the bed. Finally, the Jesuit called out the last syllables of the ritual and silence fell as Father Bishop whispered "Amen."

The room was suddenly calm and Robbie slipped down into what seemed to be a real sleep, free of the thrashing and of the nightmare that he claimed to have been experiencing. Father Bowdern slipped to his knees and prayed silently for a moment. As he did, Father Bishop glanced at his watch. It was almost 5:00 a.m.

Was it finally over? Had whatever been plaguing Robbie actually departed?

Father Bishop parted his lips to offer a prayer of gratitude to God but before he could speak, Robbie threw himself forward on the bed. His eyes were tightly closed and he hissed in a sharp breath before he began to sing. "Way down upon the Swanee River, far, far away...." he cackled, his voice very loud and high-pitched. He swung his arms about, as if directing the music, but they waved wildly, completely out of time. He then started to sing "Ole Man River, dat Ole Man River, he mus' know sumpin'" in a phony "minstrel show" accent. He garbled the shouted words, screeching and yelling.

Father Bowdern, though exhausted and near to collapse, began praying again. Father Bishop was too tired to record what prayers were said but he ended the record for this night with a note: "About 7:30 a.m., R began a natural sleep and continued quite peacefully until 1:00 p.m. of the 17th. Then he ate an ordinary meal and participated in a game of Monopoly."

The first night of the exorcism had come to an end. Despite Father Bishop's initial relief when Robbie slipped into a peaceful sleep, perhaps thinking the horror was over, he knew from the research that he and Father Bowdern that

90

exorcisms could sometimes last for months at a time. It seemed that the exorcism of "Robbie Doe" was not going to be an exception to this rule.

When the three men left the house on Roanoke Drive that morning, all of them faced a dilemma. Bowdern and Bishop explained to Walter Halloran that they had no idea how long the exorcism could last. It was possible that it could go on indefinitely and during this time, each of them had to carry out his regular duties. And thanks to Archbishop Ritter's order of secrecy, none of them would be able to reveal what they were doing or be able to use their nocturnal activities as an excuse for being tired, as all three of them certainly were on the morning of St. Patrick's Day, 1949.

None of them would have much time before their days began. Father Bowdern had an entire day of pastoral work to carry out and Father Bishop had a full schedule of classes. However, both Jesuits at least had the luxury of being somewhat independent. Walter Halloran had the most trouble to face over his involvement with the exorcism. His day usually began at 5:00 a.m. but he had less freedom than the other two men. He was still a scholastic and while he lived in a private room of a residence hall, his studies and his non-school hours were rigidly controlled. There was no way for him to be able to stay out all night without extraordinary permission.

In early 2005, I had the privilege of speaking with Father Halloran about his involvement in the case and I asked him how he managed to take part in the exorcisms at night and still function as a student during the daytime. He told me that it was not easy and that he had to get private permission from a superior priest, known as Father Minister, to be able to be away so much. He explained that Father Bowdern assisted with this. He added that he spent most of that spring nearly exhausted.

"What made you decide to continue with it?" I asked him.

"Father Bowdern asked for my help," he replied simply. "I would have never considering turning him down."

After leaving the home of Robbie's aunt and uncle that morning, Halloran quickly drove Father Bishop and Father Bowdern back to the St. Louis University campus. He managed to get back to his room, shave, shower and make it to class on time. It would not be the last time that spring that the young man would have to endure an entire day of classes without any sleep.

Later on that afternoon, Father Bowdern telephoned Robbie's family, was told of the Monopoly game and also learned that Robbie's father was returning to St. Louis from Maryland. He had been forced to go home in order to keep his job but he had a few days off and came straight to St. Louis to be with his wife and son. Robbie's mother had told her husband what had occurred during the exorcism ritual the night before and he was determined to fly into the city and be there before the Thursday night session.

On the night of March 17, Halloran drove the two Jesuits back to the house on Roanoke Drive. Robbie's mother was frantic when she met them at the door. Her husband and his brother were upstairs holding Robbie down. The three men could hear the sounds of shouting and howling coming from the second floor bedroom.

As they walked toward the stairs, Robbie's mother quickly explained what had happened. Robbie had spent an uneventful day and seemed unaffected by what had occurred the night before. Around 9:00 p.m., though, he started to get very sleepy and was almost unable to make it to the bedroom. She said that he actually fell asleep while standing up, putting on his pajamas. His mother and father who arrived late in the afternoon got him into bed but almost as soon as he was covered up, he began to shout and thrash about. It was just as he had behaved the night before.

Father Bowdern and Father Bishop put on their surplices and stoles as they ascended the staircase. Walter Halloran followed close behind them. As they walked into the bedroom, they were stunned to see Robbie's father and uncle as they held the boy down onto the bed. Robbie was kicking, scratching and swinging his arms in their grasp. He was screaming as he did so, gnashing his teeth and snapping at them like a dog.

Father Bowdern immediately went into action, sprinkling Robbie with holy water and slapping him several times across the face. The boy suddenly sat up and looked around and then his head tipped back and he slipped into unconsciousness again. His eyes rolled back into his head and he began shaking and screaming again. Father Bowdern motioned for Halloran to assist Robbie's uncle and father and Walter grabbed one of the boy's arms. Despite the burly athlete's solid grip, along with those of the other two men, the thin, slight boy still managed to rock and jerk against him. It seemed impossible that someone as small as Robbie could muster such incredible strength. It was a supernatural strength, Father Bowdern believed, a sure sign that Robbie was truly possessed.

The Jesuit quickly opened the *Rituale Romanum* and began to read the first of the prayers. As he spoke the words, Robbie became violent again. With his eyes shut tight, he turned his head and spit into the face of his father, then his uncle and Halloran. He instinctively found each of their faces, never looking even one time. As this occurred, Father Bowdern leaned down and spoke loudly over the sound of Robbie's cries. The boy retaliated by suddenly breaking free, snatching out with his hands and ripping Bowdern's stole into small pieces. Startled, Father Bishop sprinkled holy water onto Robbie's face and then sharply recoiled as the boy spit into his eyes. As his mother reached over to cool Robbie's

92

brow with a cloth, he managed to spit a large amount of liquid into her face as well.

Robbie then turned in the direction of Walter Halloran and even though he ducked out of the way, Robbie managed to spit straight into his face too. He could never explain how the boy managed to do it with his eyes closed. "He could spit right into your face from four or five feet away," Halloran told me. "We could never figure out how he managed to do it. If it was some sort of trick, it was a good one."

Even with all of this going on, Father Bowdern never wavered from the task at hand. He continued to read from the prayer book and, to their credit, Halloran and Father Bishop continued to respond on cue. In the background, Robbie's aunt, who was occasionally joined by other family members, recited the rosary.

A few times, Robbie awakened from the trance-like sleep that he was in and he looked confused whenever his father or mother asked him why he was shouting and spitting at everyone. Most of the time, though, he screamed and howled, arching his body up and down on the bed and thrashing wildly. Once in a while, he sang, loudly and off-key, in a warbling "negro voice," crooning offensive "slave songs" and tunes like "Swanee River."

Bowdern continued to read and when he finished the prayers of exorcism, he stayed at Robbie's bedside, reciting the rosary, until about 1:30 a.m. At that time, the boy finally slipped into what seemed to be a normal sleep. After he stayed at rest for some time, Father Bowdern called the exorcism at an end for the night. He led the way downstairs and waited with Walter Halloran as Father Bishop recorded everyone's recollections of the night in the "exorcist's diary." When he was finished, Halloran drove the two Jesuits back to the university and all of them retired for the night.

Father Bowdern, after a few hours of sleep, said his regular daily mass at St. Francis Xavier and, even though he was physically beaten, continued his pastoral duties during the day. He heard from Robbie's parents later that afternoon. They reported that the boy had a "spell" shortly after lunch and his father had held him down while his non-Catholic mother and Catholic aunt had recited the rosary. Robbie stopped fighting after about an hour and then seemed to return to normal.

Halloran drove Father Bowdern and Father Bishop back to the house on Roanoke Drive around 7:00 p.m. on Friday evening. The three of them chatted and played games with Robbie, who enjoyed their company very much. They had spent a couple of hours together before Robbie announced that he was getting tired and wanted to go to bed. He went upstairs to get ready and as soon as he got into bed, the priests and Halloran again gathered in his room.

Father Bowdern led the other two men in the rosary and Robbie slowly joined in. When they were finished, Father Bowdern mentioned Our Lady of Fatima, a story that Robbie had earlier enjoyed. When the priest recited a prayer specifically to Our Lady of Fatima, Robbie remained calm and awake. This was a good sign, Father Bowdern believed, that things would go well on this night.

Father Bowdern took his place on one side of the bed and Father Bishop stood on the other. Halloran again went to the end of the bed and waited. The prayer book was opened to the section on exorcism and the first prescribed prayer, the Litany of the Saints, was begun. The sound of the words filled the bedroom with Father Bowdern reciting a phrase in Latin and Father Bishop and Halloran responding.

The prayer was only beginning when the mattress of the bed began to shake. Father Bowdern stopped reading, marked his place in the prayer book and then picked up a bottle of holy water from the bedside table. He sprinkled the mattress with the water and it stopped shaking. Bowdern open the book again and the Jesuits resumed the litany.

A few moments later, Robbie exploded into spasms with his arms and legs flailing. He tore at the blankets and sheets, his body whipping up and down, back and forth on the bed. Robbie's father and uncle rushed into room and grabbed the boy's arms, just as Halloran took hold of both of his ankles. But even with all three men holding him, Robbie still managed to twist and whip-saw his body up and down until his back bowed into an arch. Father Bishop later wrote in the "exorcist's diary": "The contortions revealed physical strength beyond the natural power of R."

Robbie twisted his head back and forth and began hacking up copious amounts of spit, mixed with mucus and blood. Although his eyes were tightly closed, he never missed his intended targets. Father Bishop tried to duck but managed to be spattered anyway. He did managed to sprinkle the boy with holy water, though, and Robbie screeched and writhed when the water hit him, as if in pain. Bowdern wrote: "He fought and screamed in a diabolical, high-pitched voice."

Father Bowdern stopped reading and, as instructed in the *Rituale Romanum*, he tried to touch Robbie with a holy relic. Robbie spat on it and then spun and managed to spit on Father Bishop's upraised hand. Father Bowdern reached under his surplice and took a small gold box from a pocket inside of his cassock. In the box was a round wafer, the consecrated host that is revered as the Blessed Sacrament, the body of Christ, during Holy Communion. Robbie's feet were moving on the mattress, pounding against the foot board of the bed as if stomping up a long flight of stairs. Father Bowdern held the gold box near the sole of one of the spastic feet and it suddenly stopped moving, even though the other leg continued to jerk in time with the march.

A moment later, Robbie was conscious. He complained that his arms were sore and one by one, he looked at his father, uncle and his new friend, Walter Halloran. He seemed to sense that the three of them were responsible for the soreness but he said nothing about it. Robbie smiled humorlessly at them before his eyes rolled back into his head again and he flung himself back down onto the bed. He let out a horrific scream and his body again began to thump up and down as if he were being picked up and then slammed down by unseen hands.

Father Bowdern continued the prayers and occasionally, Robbie would come out of his trance and attempt to respond to the litany with Father Bishop and Halloran. At one point, he calmed down enough that his captors released him. In that instant, Robbie went into a rage. According to Father Bishop's "exorcist's diary":

R stood up in bed and fought all of those around him. He shouted, jumped and swung his fists. His face was devilish and he snapped his teeth in fury. He snapped at the Priest's hands in the blessings. He bit those who held him.

Robbie was wrestled back down onto the bed and he resumed fighting and spitting as the prayers wore on. He fluctuated between frenzy and calm for the next several hours and then, as the clock was reaching midnight, his body and face relaxed. The three exhausted men who had been holding him collapsed in relief.

In an instant, the boy sprang to his feet. In the middle of the bed, he dropped to his knees and bent so far forward that his forehead touched the mattress. After a few moments of silence, he began to chant "Our Lady of Fatima, pray for us" and then he began to recite the Hail Mary. While everyone in the room was frozen into place, spellbound by what they were seeing, he abruptly stood again and began, in Father Bishop's words, "his strong fight for the eviction of the Devil." The diary continued:

His gyrations were in all directions. He pulled off the upper part of his underwear, and held his arms high above himself in supplication. Then he made as though he was trying to vomit from his stomach. His gestures moved upwards, close to his body. He seemed to try and lift the devil from his stomach to his throat.

Robbie cried for someone to open the window and one of his relatives threw up the sash. Cold winds whipped into the room, snapping the cloth of the curtains as Robbie screamed again. "He's going! He's going!" the boy cried. "There he goes!" As these words echoed into the night, Robbie collapsed onto the bed, his body limp and soaked with sweat.

All of those gathered in the room knelt down and Father Bowdern led a prayer of thanks. Robbie's mother wept tears of joy. Robbie told everyone what he had experienced. According to the boy, he had seen a huge black stain that had clouded his vision. Inside of the darkness, he had seen a terrible figure in a black cowl who had turned and started to walk away from him. The figure grew smaller and smaller and then suddenly, it disappeared. The long nightmare, it seemed, was finally over.

Robbie left his bed and smiling happily, he put on his robe and went downstairs with the three Jesuits. He talked with them for a few minutes and then said good bye to them at about 1:30 a.m. Father Bowdern, Father Bishop and Walter Halloran, relieved and feeling joyous over the events of the evening, drove back to the university and bid one another good night.

Father Bowdern walked to the rectory and after his prayers, climbed into bed. He was soon fast asleep. At 3:15 a.m., however, the rectory telephone jangled him awake. Dreading what he was going to hear, Father Bowdern picked up the receiver to find Robbie on the other end of the line. His screams were horrifying as they came over the line. "He's coming back!" the boy cried.

Father Bowdern stumbled back to his room and hurriedly got dressed. Careful not to awaken anyone in the residence hall, he quietly knocked on the door of Walter Halloran's room. The young man had just gotten into bed and he later recalled that Father Bowdern said "We're going to go again." He didn't have to say anything else. Halloran knew that they were going back to Roanoke Drive.

After rounding up Father Bishop, the three men drove back to the house. Without speaking, they ascended the stairs and filed into Robbie's bedroom. It was as though the final events of earlier in the evening had never occurred at all. Father Bowdern began to recite the prayers of exorcism as Robbie writhed on the bed, howling and screaming in agony. The ritual continued for the next several hours until, around 7:30 a.m., Robbie fell into what seemed to be a peaceful and natural sleep.

The three men departed from the house once more and drove back to the university in uneasy silence. For the first time, Walter Halloran reported many years later, the Jesuits actually felt despair. They wondered if the horror would ever really end at all.

Saturday arrived with a normalcy that was almost disconcerting on its own. Robbie played, read comic books, listened to the radio and acted like an ordinary young boy. As the day grew later, though, and night began to fall, Robbie's mood

96

became darker and as he readied for bed, everyone knew the terror would come. On Saturday night, Father Bowdern tried to push the dark period into an earlier hour, thus sparing not only the family, but the exorcists and their assistant, a nightlong battle. If they could get Robbie into bed by 8:00 p.m. or so, perhaps the ordeal could be ended by midnight rather than during the early morning hours.

The Jesuits arrived at the house on Roanoke Drive just before 7:00 p.m. and they spent the next hour calmly interacting with the family and easing Robbie into bed. After he had settled in, Father Bowdern and the others entered the room. Soon, the exorcism began again and Robbie started to fight against Walter Halloran as he tried to hold the boy down on the bed. Father Bowdern read and Father Bishop responded. Robbie responded in his own way by barking like a dog.

As Bowdern read "I command thee, unclean spirit...." And then asked in Latin for the spirit to "show some sign", Robbie provided a sign by urinating all over the bed, something he had never done before. The urine sprayed the blankets and sheets, creating an overpowering stench in the room. Father Bowdern commanded that the demon give his name and Robbie urinated again. Father Bowdern then asked for the demon's hour of departure and once more, urine streamed from Robbie's body, soaking his pajamas and the bed.

Father Bowdern refused to acknowledge the urinating and as he prayed, he stepped forward and made the sign of the cross on the boy's brow, lips and chest. The urinating suddenly stopped. Father Bowdern made the sign of the cross over Robbie again and he placed the end of the stole on the boy's neck. He placed a strong hand on Robbie's head as he continued to pray and the boy seemed to calm from his touch. The shouting and barking stopped, at least for the moment. Then, he began to sign again.

This time, it was not an offensive imitation of a minstrel show but the careful, clear notes of the "Blue Danube Waltz." It was beautiful rendered and unbelievably bright and Robbie's hands kept time, swinging up and down. It was the voice of a choirboy and to Father Bishop, who had an ear for music, a seemingly trained voice. However, he knew this was not the case, at least with Robbie. After the previous outbursts, Father Bishop had asked Robbie's mother about the boy's musical abilities. His mother told the priest that Robbie could not sing well and in fact, had never liked to sing at all. This was understandable from his previous poor performances but not on this night.

A few moments later, Robbie began singing the familiar hymn, "The Old Rugged Cross." Although his performance was excellent, and to Father Bishop, of professional quality, this time Robbie's voice was mocking and almost cruel. Then, the signing stopped. Robbie awakened for a moment as he often did during the exorcism ritual and Father Bishop asked him to hum along with the

97

tune of the "Blue Danube Waltz." Robbie claimed that he did not know the song and when Father Bishop hummed it for him, he was unable to carry the melody on his own.

Robbie slipped back into his trance a few minutes later. As Father Bowdern continued his prayers, Robbie called out to one of the priests by name. Father Bishop did not record which of them it was in the "exorcist's diary" but regardless, the priest did not respond to him. According to the *Rituale Romanum*, exorcists are advised against conversing directly with the demon because the spirit will attempt to distract them so that they can keep the ritual from being carried out. So, when Robbie called out to the priest again even though his voice was pleasant , he was ignored once more. Finally, he hissed out the priest's name in a harsh voice and added "you stink!" While this is a pretty tame insult by most standards, the reader must remember that this would have been completely against Robbie's usual nature, especially when addressing one of the Jesuits, men he liked very much. The priests and Walter Halloran would remember this because it would become the first of what would be increasingly vehement personal attacks against the three of them.

The anger with the priest started another episode of violence from Robbie, which Halloran struggled to control. The shouting and thrashing continued until 3:00 a.m., when Robbie finally slipped into a deep sleep that Father Bowdern judged to be natural. He, Father Bishop and Halloran waited and prayed by the boy's bed for about another half an hour before they left.

After that, Robbie's family began another nightly ritual: removing the bed sheets and pajamas of the sleeping boy and exchanging them with fresh ones. On night's past, the sheets and clothing had been soaked with sweat but now, with all of the urine, he had to be washed as well.

On Sunday night, Father Bowdern began the prayer ritual at 8:00 p.m. and within a few minutes, this night was shaping up to be the worst one so far. Robbie cursed and threw himself about on the bed, cursing, screaming and threatening Walter Halloran. He sprayed urine all over the bed and passed gas loudly. The room began to stink so badly that, even though it was a cold night, the window had to be opened to air the place out. Years later, Father Halloran told me that the stench was so bad that it could make their eyes water. "Keep in mind that I served as a chaplain with hundreds of young men in Vietnam," he told me. "I have seen and have smelled just about everything that you can imagine but I'll never forget the odors in that boy's room, both at the house and later at the hospital. I can't even begin to describe it."

Soon, Robbie curses turned from Halloran to the priests. "Get away from me, you assholes!" he screamed at them. His voice would range from a high-pitched squeal to a guttural roar. During the course of the exorcism, various witnesses would describe Robbie's voice in different ways. Some said that it was deep and menacing --- much too deep to come from a young boy not yet through puberty. Others recalled it as high-pitched and screeching, like fingernails on a chalkboard. Others could never get his repetitive, jangling laughter out of their heads.

All of them would remember the vile curses that flew from his lips, words that no one could remember Robbie ever using before this. "Go to hell!" he railed at the priests. "You're dirty sons of bitches! You goddamn assholes!"

Even though Father Bowdern never reacted to the curses and swearing, Father Bishop was shocked and never recorded much of what Robbie said. He simply wrote that the curses were too offensive to be put to paper. Much of what he said described sexual acts with various people, the Blessed Mother and more. He cleverly wove sexual images into prayers to Our Lady of Fatima and perverted the rosary and other prayers. Robbie's parents swore that he had no prior knowledge of the filthy images that he described and suggested.

The cursing and fighting ended at 2:00 a.m. and by this time, Robbie's aunt and uncle could take no more. The next morning, on March 21, Robbie's mother, who was near to collapse from fear and lack of sleep, was taken to a doctor. She never told him the reason for her exhaustion but he prescribed immediate rest.

Robbie was oblivious as to what was going on. He remembered nothing of his nightly frenzies, which baffled everyone. They couldn't imagine that he could act as he did and do the things that he did without remembering them. But according to Walter Halloran, they believed his amnesia to be genuine. "He never referred to anything that he did and I never had the feeling that he was putting on an act," he said.

Robbie was a fine young man during the daylight hours but at night, he was a terror -- and becoming more horrific each night. Although they loved their nephew, his aunt and uncle had reached the limits of their endurance. They were relieved, although they felt guilty about it, to hear that Father Bowdern and Father Bishop recommended removing Robbie from their home. The Jesuits suggested that he be placed in a hospital, at least for a night, so that the rest of the family could sleep and not be awakened by screams and struggling. Robbie was not consulted about the situation, although his parents agreed to whatever recommendations the Jesuits might have.

Father Bowdern made arrangements for Robbie to be taken to the Alexian Brothers Hospital, an institution that as well known in the city and a place that would achieve the status of legend in the story of the 1949 St. Louis Exorcism.

The old Alexian Brothers hospital in South St. Louis

The Alexian Brothers Hospital was built by an order called the Congregation of Cellites. The order was founded by monks who cared for victims of the Black Death, which swept through Europe in the fourteenth century. They were often known as the Poor Brothers, or Bread Brothers, who cared for the dying and the mad and who stayed behind to bury the dead after others fled from the plague. The order's patron saint, St. Alexius, was a holy man who devoted his life to helping the poor.

The Alexians opened their first hospital in Chicago in 1866, specializing in the treatment of "idiots and lunatics of the male sex." The Brothers continued this specialty when they opened their hospital in St. Louis in 1869 and shocked the segregated, race-conscious city by promising to treat men of "any class, nationality, religion, race or color." On December 7 of that year, the Simmons Mansion on Carondolet Road now South Broadway at Osage Street, which had been purchased by the Brothers from Mr. James Lucas, was blessed as St. Joseph's Hospital. Patients were not admitted to the hospital until April 1870.

A rather large addition to the building was completed in 1874 and the original mansion became the "Insane Department," which was the first psychiatric division in any general hospital in St. Louis. There were strict rules that forbid the use of chains, handcuffs and straitjackets but violent patients could be placed in "security rooms." Father Bowdern arranged for one of these security rooms on the fifth floor of the building in 1949 when he checked Robbie into the hospital.

100

On March 21, just after 10:00 p.m., Robbie was admitted to the hospital and put to bed in one of the security rooms. Although Father Bowdern was well aware of the demand for secrecy that had been placed on the exorcism, he was trusting of the Alexians. The order was among the first medical practitioners in America to recognize alcoholism as a disease and since the 1920s, had treated alcoholics. In addition, they also secretly cared for alcoholic priests and were given the responsibility for deciding when they were cured and able to resume their duties. This highly guarded secret insured Father Bowdern that the brothers could be entrusted with his secret as well.

The security room must have been a disconcerting place for Robbie. There were leather straps on his bed, bars on the windows and no doorknob on the inside of the door. The only way to get out of the room was to knock on the door until one of the brothers let you out. The room itself was sparsely furnished. There was a single bed with an iron frame, a nightstand, a desk and chair and a small couch that one of the brothers moved into the room for Robbie's father, who had expressed his wish to stay the night with his son.

Robbie nervously entered the room and say down on the bed. He seemed unnerved by his surroundings -- perhaps more disconcerted by the place than by the reason he was there. Father Bowdern began reciting the Litany of the Saints, the prelude to the exorcism, and Father Bishop and Walter Halloran braced themselves for another long night of terror. But then nothing happened. Robbie was not asleep -- or in his usual trance -- and in fact, his eyes were open in fear and he was looking wildly at the room, the bars on the windows and the leather straps that had been fastened on his wrists. The boy was terrified and unusually quiet.

For the first time, the exorcism went on without any interruptions from Robbie, who remained awake the entire time. When the prayers ended, Father Bowdern led everyone in the room, including several Alexian brothers, in the rosary. Then, he quietly rapped on the door so that they could leave. Father Bowdern led the way and gestured for everyone but Robbie's father to follow. As they left, Father Bishop glanced back to see Robbie's father leaning over his son, comforting him and soothing him to sleep. He later told Father Bishop that Robbie fell into a deep and untroubled sleep at about 11:30 p.m. His father laid down on the couch and for the first time in several months, both he and his son slept peacefully.

The next morning, Robbie woke up around 6:30 a.m. and awakened his father. After getting dressed and getting their few things together, they left the hospital and returned to the house on Roanoke Drive. They spent the day there without incident and for the first time, the family began to feel a glimmer of hope.

Father Bowdern was pleased by the successful night. He hoped that Robbie was beginning to recover and with that in mind, decided that one night in the hospital was enough for the boy. The next night, Tuesday, March 22, Robbie remained at the house on Roanoke Drive. Around 9:30 p.m., a little while after Robbie had gone to bed, the mattress on the bed began to shake and the boy again slipped into his chilling trance.

Robbie's mother immediately called Father Bishop, who hurried to the house in the company of two priests that he did not identify but one of them was likely his friend, Father Kenny . The three men knelt around the shaking bed and recited the prayers of exorcism, followed by the rosary. Shortly before midnight, Robbie began to breathe deeply as he faded into deep, natural sleep. Father Bishop and the other two priests left the house and returned to the university, where Bishop informed Father Bowdern what had occurred.

He was not as concerned about the relapse as one might believe. He interpreted Robbie's more docile behavior as a sign that the possession was easing, so Father Bowdern decided to take things one step further and attempt to convert Robbie to Catholicism. He believed that such a decision would bring Robbie into the ranks of the Church, which was his greatest form of protection against the negative entities that were assailing him. With Robbie "aiding in his own defense," so to speak, the priests stood a much better chance of ridding the boy of the problem. Father Bowdern spoke to his parents about this and Robbie's father, who had been born and baptized in the Church, readily consented to have his son instructed as a Catholic.

On Wednesday, Father Bowdern set up a room in the St. Francis Xavier rectory where Robbie and his father could stay. That afternoon, Father Bowdern spent several hours talking to Robbie about Catholicism and teaching him prayers that Catholic children learned as a sort of primer to the faith. These four prayers ---- the Acts of Faith, Hope, Love and Contrition ---- were the essentials of the Catholic faith and, as Father Bowdern believed, a weapon for a boy who was possessed.

At 9:30 p.m., Robbie went to bed in the rectory room. Father Bowdern, Father Bishop, Walter Halloran and Robbie's father all gathered in the room and they were joined by a newcomer to the exorcism, Father William A. Van Roo, S.J., a priest who had already been ordained and was now working on his internship of religious work.

Father Van Roo was considered brilliant, even by other Jesuits, and he had already started his life's work as a theologian by studying the influences of Arabian philosophy on Thomas Aquinas. He would go on to become an eminent theologian on the faculty of the Gregorian University in Rome but in March 1949, he was recruited as a possible assistant for Father Bowdern. He had been assigned to work with Father Bowdern at the church as part of his internship but the older priest had sworn him to secrecy and brought him along to help with Robbie.

Everyone gathered in the room joined Robbie in reciting the Acts of Faith, Hope, Love and Contrition and then Father Bowdern began the Litany of the Saints. Robbie instantly exploded! He began to scream, kicking and swinging at Halloran, who pressed the boy onto the bed and called for Van Roo and the boy's father to help him. As Bowdern prayed, the three men struggled to hold Robbie, who continued to twist and fight. He screamed and howled for several minutes and then grew very quiet. His eyes, which had been tightly clenched shut, opened up and he smiled up at Walter Halloran. When Robbie spoke, his voice was completely normal. It was as though the last few minutes had never happened at all. "Please let go of my arms," he said to Halloran in a subdued tone. "You're hurting me."

Halloran faltered. "I'm just going to hold my hands close to you," he replied. He eased his hands away from Robbie's thin arms and Father Van Roo did the same. He frowned as he let go.

But Robbie's docile mood abruptly ended with a howling scream and Halloran snatched up the boy's arm again. Father Van Roo did the same, pouncing forward and pressing it to the mattress. He hesitated to hold it very hard, though. He looked sharply over at Halloran and frowned at the young man. "There is no sense in holding his arms that hard," Father Van Roo said. "You are only making him uncomfortable."

Halloran started to object. He had been through this with Robbie several times before and this was the first time that Van Roo had dealt with it. However, he also realized that the other man was a priest and that Halloran was only a scholastic. Following Father Van Roo's orders, Halloran let go of Robbie's arm.

In a split second, Robbie -- with his eyes closed -- lashed out and slammed a fist into Halloran's nose, which broke with a loud snap. With his other hand, he swung and back-handed Van Roo in the face as well. The priest's nose exploded with a gush of blood but at least it wasn't broken. Father Van Roo blinked with pain and reached out to take hold of Robbie's swinging arm. Walter Halloran had already pinned the other arm back down on the bed. This time, he was not letting go -- no matter who told him to do so. Father Van Roo finally realized that Halloran was not intentionally hurting the boy and he too grimly bore down on Robbie's arms.

As Father Bowdern continued to recite the exorcism prayers, Robbie began to urinate and break wind, laughing and screaming as he did so. The smell in the room became so overpowering that Robbie's father ran for the window and flung it open.

One of the great legends surrounding the St. Louis Exorcism concerned the sounds and smells reported from the rectory during the time that Robbie was there. Near the rectory was Verhaegen Hall, an old brick residence building that was filled with private Jesuit rooms. Scholastics, like Walter Halloran, lived on the first floor. Priests in their studies for doctorates and those on the university faculty lived on the second and third floors. As the years have passed, many stories have emerged and all of them claim to be first-person recollections from priests who lived in Verhaegen Hall. In every story, the priests claimed to remember hearing diabolical screams and evil laughter coming from the rectory or managed to catch a whiff of some foul odor. No one knows whether these tales come from a single memory, often repeated, or whether many of the priests actually noticed something odd. They would have known nothing at the time, thanks to the secrecy surrounding the case, but they likely would have been curious. According to one of the priests, who was up late studying one night: "I heard this wild, idiotic, diabolical laughter. I looked toward the window from where the light was coming, but saw nothing."

As Halloran and Van Roo were fighting Robbie and his father was assisting in whatever way he could, Father Bowdern and Father Bishop were experiencing the worst night so far. The two men were tortured by the fact that Robbie would awaken from his trance occasionally, whimpering and weeping, and then would plunge back into unconsciousness, laughing and screaming. "I'm in hell," he cried and then turned to Father Bowdern. "I see you! I see you ---- you're in hell. It's 1957!"

For the first time in the exorcism, Father Bowdern reacted to one of the things that Robbie said. His prayer faltered and his face turned pale. He looked around for a moment, confused and tormented, but then turned back to the prayer book, renewed once more.

Robbie continued to scream and laugh, describing his penis and the anatomy of the other men in the room. A towel had been draped across his body to soak up the urine and he managed to slip his hands free, toss aside the towel and pretend to masturbate. Father Van Roo and Halloran grabbed his hands and pinned them to the mattress again. He continued to shout, bawling out words that Father Bishop refused to record. He only noted that they were "lowly and smacked of the abuse of sex." He also remarked that Robbie, during his periods of daytime normalcy, never used obscene words.

The screaming, obscenities and violence continued for the next several hours, wearing on the Jesuits gathered in the room and on especially on Robbie's father. His son had never been a perfect child but the "monster" in this bedroom was

104

unrecognizable to him. Robbie drifted in and out of his "eyes-closed" state, barking like a dog, singing strange songs and contorting suggestively. Finally, at about 2:30 a.m., his body went limp and he fell into a natural sleep.

The horrific night was over but the possession continued on.

When it was over, Walter Halloran limped back to his room and collapsed into his bed. His nose was sore it would turn out to be broken and he hoped that none of his advisors or the other scholastics would ask him about it. He had to be up again at 5:00 a.m. and go about his duties, attend his classes and remain awake through his meditations and masses. He continued with his studies and each night, returned to Robbie's room and continued assisting with the exorcism.

Father Bishop was in a similar state of mind, going through the motions of class and study each day and then plunging into the terror of the exorcism at night. He wondered how long it could go on -- the same thing day after day, the same prayers, the same hopes raised and then dashed again when the evil refused to leave the boy. Father Bishop knew, as did Halloran, that despair and doubt would do nothing to help Robbie and he made a solid effort to shake the uneasiness from his mind.

As for Father Bowdern, he was troubled, but he never despaired, even after the terrifying first night at the rectory. He believed that the departure of the demon was imminent, convinced that the spirit had revealed when he would leave days before. During the exorcism, the prayer ritual called for the demon to reveal when it would depart. On the first night, when a jagged "X" had appeared on Robbie's leg, both priests had decided that this was a sign that the demon would leave Robbie in ten days. Father Bishop believed that the day of departure would be Thursday, March 24, because it was the Feast of St. Gabriel, the archangel who was so high in the Litany of Saints. Father Bowdern disagreed and believed that the say would be Friday, March 25. He also pointed out that this day was the Feast of Annunciation, exactly nine months before Christmas, when the Archangel Gabriel said "Hail Mary" and announced to the Blessed Mother the incarnation of Christ.

Robbie remained at the rectory on Thursday and that night, with Father Bishop still confident that the terror would end, Father Bowdern again started the litany. He had just spoken the name of Gabriel when Robbie began to let out a bloodcurdling scream. He shouted, barked, howled and began to break wind and urinate all over the bed. The bed chamber was again filled with a foul odor that made the eyes of the men in the room start to water. Robbie's father again threw open the window so they could breathe.

Father Bowdern had invited several other Jesuits to assist them with the exorcism, although Father Bishop does not record their names in the "exorcist's diary." One of them, a man who was somewhat overweight, was singled out for special abuse by Robbie. He helped Walter Halloran hold the boy down during the worst of his seizures and Robbie screamed at him and called him a "fat ass" and an "ox." He also told the man that he "had big teats" and made sucking sounds whenever he came near. During one of the violent spasms, Robbie also told the man that he "would be with me in hell in 1957." According to one of the stories that circulated about the exorcism, the priest, who had always been a heavy drinker, swore off alcohol for months.

Father Bishop made a note in the "diary" that Robbie's foulest words came after midnight, desecrating the Feast of Annunciation. He screamed about "kissing my pecker" and "using my stick" and accused the priests of having larges penises that "you like to rub up and down." He bellowed for the priests to "cut out the damned Latin" and to "get away from me, you goddamn bastards!" Robbie also made other suggestive and filthy comments that Father Bishop refused to transcribe. One of them, recalled years later by Walter Halloran, involved Father Bowdern. Robbie turned his blind eyes to the priest and said "You like to stay with me. Well, I like it too." When Father Bowdern ignored him, Robbie resumed his vicious cursing and thrashing.

One of the Jesuits who was present that night may have been Father Charles O'Hara of Marquette University in Milwaukee. There is no other record of him being involved with the exorcism at least by name in Father Bishop's "diary" but since he did claim to witness some of the happenings in the case, we have to surmise that he visited the rectory when Robbie was there. Years later, Father O'Hara would pass along what he saw to Father Eugene Gallagher of Georgetown University in Washington. At the time, Father Gallagher was teaching a class about exorcisms that had been performed by Jesus and one of the students in the class was a future writer named William Peter Blatty. More about this later in the book

According to Father Gallagher, Father O'Hara passed on one of the most dramatic incidents connected to the case. He stated: "One night, the boy brushed off his handlers and soared through the air at Father Bowdern standing at some distance from his bed with the ritual book in his hands. Presumably, the Father was about to be attacked but the boy got no further than the book. And when his hands hit that ---- I assure you, Gene, I saw it with my own eyes ---- he didn't tear the book, he dissolved it! The book vaporized into confetti and fell in fine small pieces all over the floor."

The horrifying events continued for the next two hours or so and then at around 2:30 a.m., Robbie calmed down and sank down into a genuine sleep. Relieved, the men did the best that they could to clean up Robbie and the room without waking the boy. Then, Father Bishop and Halloran, along with that night's assistants, headed back to the residence hall, leaving Robbie's father and Father Bowdern alone. When Father Bowdern went wearily to bed, he did so with the confidence that the possession was nearly at an end. Tomorrow, he thought, he would order the demon's to depart and they would finally leave Robbie's body once and for all.

Robbie slept until 11:30 a.m. on the morning of March 25. He rose to start another of his normal days, about which Father Bishop kept almost no record. He was more concerned about what took place during the evening sessions and so he wrote only about what happened to the boy at night. It's likely that he was left mostly to his own devices during the day. There is no record that his mother ever visited the rectory Jesuit residences were usually off limits to members of the opposite sex and Robbie spent most days reading and keeping to himself. Father Bowdern spent as much time with him as he could, continuing to instruct him in the Catholic faith and giving him books to read. Robbie learned to like and trust Father Bowdern but, despite his friendly relationships with Father Bishop and Walter Halloran, he never trusted or cared for them as he did the older priest.

As darkness fell on the evening of March 25, Father Bowdern prepared for what he felt would be the end of Robbie's ordeal. Soon after Robbie went to his bedroom, Jesuit priests invited by Father Bowdern began arriving at the rectory. When Father Bowdern, Father Bishop, Father Van Roo, Walter Halloran and Robbie's father gathered in the room with the boy, other Jesuits gathered outside the door of the room to pray.

As the men inside of the room began to pray, Robbie began to toss and turn on the bed. He slipped into one of his trances and without cursing, screaming or making any other sound, he began to physically act very strangely. Lying flat on his back, he stiffly moved his arms in and out from his sides, while he scissored his legs back and forth at the same time. It was as though his body was moving involuntarily but he showed no effort as he did so. His face remained impassive and completely calm for several minutes and then the movements became faster and faster. Walter Halloran attempted to halt the movement but he was unable to do so. The boy's arms and legs slammed against him as they began swinging faster and faster. Finally, Robbie's body convulsed out of control and he fell from the bed and crashed to the floor.

Robbie stayed completely still on the hardwood floor and Halloran gently lifted him back into the bed. As soon as he was laid back down, the movements began again. This time, as the speed increased, he rolled off the bed and into the arms of Father Van Roo. The priest lifted the boy back into the bed again and the movements stopped. Robbie now was completely silent and calm. The tension

107

in the room was palpable, though --- Robbie had not slipped into a normal sleep. Something was going to happen, they all knew, but could not imagine what it would be.

It was just after midnight when the mood in the room changed again. Robbie broke his silence by cursing his father and spitting into the man's face. He had been so quiet that Halloran and Father Van Roo had relaxed their grip on him. Robbie bolted away from them and swung his body around on the bed so that he could deliver solid kicks to his father and to Father Bowdern, who grunted from the violence of the assault. Both men managed to get clear of the next kicks and Robbie connected with a wooden chair instead, sending it clattering across the room. Moments after this outburst, though, Robbie went into a natural sleep.

Unlike previous nights, Father Bowdern chose to continue the exorcism rather than call the proceedings to a halt. He sensed a chance for victory on a night that he still believed would mark the end of the possession. He swept his hand in the sign of the cross and persisted with the prayers, using his surplice to make additional signs of the cross over the boy as he slept. He read:

We cast thee out, every unclean spirit, every devilish power, every assault of the infernal adversary, every legion, every diabolical group and sect, by the name and power of our Lord Jesus Christ, and command thee to fly far from the Church of God and from all who are made to the image of God and redeemed by the Precious Blood of the Divine Lamb.

Presume never again, thou cunning serpent, to deceive the human race, to persecute the Church of God, nor to strike the chosen of God and sift them as wheat. For the Most High God commands thee, He to whom thou didst hitherto in thy great pride presume thyself equal; He who desireth that all men might be saved, and to come to the knowledge of truth. God the Father commandeth thee! God the Son commandeth thee! God the Holy Spirit commandeth thee! The majesty of Christ commands thee, the Eternal Word of God made flesh, who for the salvation of our race, lost through thine envy, humbled Himself and was made obedient even until death; who built his Church upon a solid rock, and proclaimed that the gates of hell should never prevail against her, and that He would remain with her all days, even to the end of the world!

Father Bowdern continued to read and he began to be filled with hope as he did so. Over the course of the exorcism so far, there had been violent reactions from Robbie whenever the Latin words of *Dominus*, *Jesu* and *Deus* had been used in the prayers. He wondered if this might be a sign that the demon had already departed. As he read, he turned to the prayer of hope, a prayer that was directed to God. Father Bowdern had his own hope that, moments before the

108

Feast of Annunciation had ended, the demon had fled from Robbie's body. He read through the prayer and when he was finished, the word "Amen" was echoed in the room by the other men present.

Father Bowdern sprinkled the bed with holy water and then led the others out of the room. The priests gathered outside simply watched as Father Bowdern walked past them. He was as exhausted as he always was, but this time he felt a calmness that he had not experienced at any time during the exorcism so far.

Robbie slept until the late hours of Saturday morning. When he awoke, he showered and dressed and his father drove him to his uncle's house on Roanoke Drive. Robbie seemed his usual complacent, daytime self but his family all watched him nervously. They knew that Father Bowdern believed the "X" meant then days and they hoped that he was right. If Robbie could get through the night without incident, they were convinced that everything would be okay.

That night, after dinner, the family had a celebration of sorts and played a game or two with the boy. His mother watched and worried over the clock, though. Finally, when she could wait no longer, she instructed Robbie to go and get ready for bed. He went upstairs, put on his pajamas and climbed into bed. His mother tucked him in and turned out the light and waited for the strange noises and violent sounds to start. She kept the telephone close to where she was sitting, convinced that she would soon be on the line with Father Bowdern, begging him to come back to the house.

She waited, looking up the stairs -- but nothing happened.

Robbie slept through the entire night and woke early to spend the day with his family. On Sunday night, again, nothing happened. Robbie and his family spent the night in peace once more. On Monday morning, Robbie's father went back to Maryland and his wife and son began making plans to follow him.

Later on that day, Father Bowdern dropped by to bless the house. He went from room to room, making the sign of the cross and sprinkling holy water. It was a day of celebration and joy, as far as he was concerned. He sat down and spoke with Robbie about his future and cautiously asked him if he was "feeling any different" now, compared to say how he had been feeling over the past few weeks. Robbie just seemed confused and puzzled by the question. He had been feeling fine, he told Father Bowdern, except for being sleepy some days, as if he had not gotten enough sleep.

On Monday afternoon, Robbie's mother began to make preparations for returning to Maryland. Train tickets were purchased and after the next two days also passed uneventfully, Robbie's relatives began looking forward to getting their home and lives back to normal again.

On Thursday night, Robbie and his cousin went to bed. Things were now more like they used to be when Robbie and his parents came to visit. The two boys laughed and horsed around and were scolded by their mothers for making so much noise. After the boys were settled down, the adults gathered in the living room to read, chat and listen to the radio. Around 11:30 p.m., they were about to go to bed themselves when Robbie came downstairs and told his mother that he was feeling sick. She told him to go back to bed and try to sleep but Robbie insisted that he was scared. His feet were hot and then cold and he wanted everyone to come back upstairs with him.

Please come, he begged them.

The adults, as well as Robbie's cousin, who had originally brought Father Bishop into the situation, looked at each other anxiously. They could not help but wonder whether or not the strange happenings were starting all over again. They followed Robbie upstairs, their hearts filled with dread.

Robbie climbed into bed but he did not lay down. His eyes clouded over and then his head dropped back. He seemed to be going into one of his trances again. As he sat there on the bed, the index finger of his hand began tracing some sort of pattern on the sheet that covered the bed. Moments later, the mattress began to shake, just as it had so many times before. Robbie kept moving his finger back and forth, as if he was writing something. He lowered his head so that his closed eyes looked down directly at the sheet, as if there was something to see there. He seemed to be reading whatever it was that he had written on the bed.

As his lips began to move, his cousin grabbed a notebook and pencil from the desk. As Robbie began to speak in a dull and monotone voice, she wrote down everything that he said. He spoke each line like it was a verse from a poem and she wrote it down just as he said it:

I will stay 10 days, but will return in 4 days
If Robbie's real name stays... gone to lunch
If you stay and become a Catholic it will stay away
*   Robbie's mother's name*
God will take it away 4 days after it has gone 10 days
God is getting powerful
The last day when it quits it will leave a sign on my front
Father Bishop
All people that mangle with me will die a terrible death

Robbie's mother left the room in tears and went downstairs to ring the rectory. When she had Father Bowdern on the telephone, she told him what had happened and read the statements that Robbie's cousin had written down. Father

110

Bowdern told her that he would be right over. He arrived just after 1:00 a.m., having been driven to the house by Walter Halloran. Perhaps disturbed by the comments that had been passed on about Father Bishop, he chose not to bring the priest with him. He came with Father Van Roo instead.

Robbie was stretched out on the bed when Father Bowdern and Father Van Roo entered the room. Father Bowdern looked over the messages that had been written and while tempted to ask about them, he recalled the warnings in the *Rituale Romanum* about engaging in conversation with the demon and started the prayers of exorcism instead.

As he was reading, he was suddenly interrupted by Robbie, who asked him for a pencil. Father Bowdern hesitated. He did not want to have a conversation with the demon but this was different. It would only be a conversation if Father Bowdern was foolish enough to write a response. As long as he did not answer whatever Robbie wrote down, it would be safe. But refusing to interrupt the prayers of exorcism, which is what the demon could be trying to do, he signaled to Father Van Roo to give the boy a pencil.

Robbie began to write and as he did so, he muttered to himself. They heard the names "Pete" and "Joe" used repeatedly and while he mumbled the words, along with other things, he started writing quickly on the bed sheet. In a frenzy, he scrawled all over the cloth as his cousin tried to keep a record of what he was writing. She jotted the messages into a notebook while Robbie was scratching them into sometimes unreadable letters.

Someone and it is not made clear in the "diary" who did this and why they did it ran out of the room, got soap and water and began washing off the sheet. The incidents that occurred on this night are fragmented in the "diary," mostly because Father Bishop was not present and based his entry on the recollections of those who were. The account describes a bizarre scene that almost went out of control. On previous nights, Father Bowdern remained calmly separate from the incidents that were occurring. He was the exorcist, steadfastly reading from the prayer book as others tried to control Robbie as he screamed and fought wildly. On this night, the people in the room, were enthralled by Robbie's behavior and rather serve as witnesses, became a part of the events.

Robbie's uncle, who ran a print shop, left the room and came back with several large sheets of paper. He tacked them up on the wall above the bed and Robbie, without hesitation, went from the bed sheet to the paper and continued writing there.

There was no mention of Father Bowdern in this account, or of the prayers of exorcism. The *Rituale Romanum* warns that "sometimes the devil will leave the possessed person... to make it appear that he has departed. In fact, the arts and fraud of the evil one for deceiving a man are innumerable. For this reason

111

the exorcist must be on his guard, lest he fall into this trap." Father Bowdern had been deceived and his hopes for the letter "X" to be the Feast of Annunciation were now shattered in the chaos of the room. He must have been admonishing himself for allowing his hopes to turn to a belief -- a belief that had undermined the exorcism. And now, a pencil had proved the undoing of this night's work. The exorcism was now out of control.

Father Bowdern, realizing what was happened, composed himself and resumed the ritual. Robbie continued his madness for nearly two more hours, slipped out of the spell and, as he usually did, fell into an untroubled sleep. When the prayers ended, Father Bowdern and the others recited the rosary and then the priest gathered the marked bed sheet and the pages of notes that Robbie's cousin had compiled. She had written down everything she could --- even though many words, phrases and remarks had been lost -- and now the Jesuits had a record of not what others had seen but what had been pulled from Robbie's own mind.

In the days to come, Father Bowdern, along with Father Bishop and Father Van Roo, studied the notes and Father Bishop arranged them for the "diary." He focused his writing on the answers to the commands that were given in the exorcism prayer: "Thou shalt tell me by some sign or other thy name and the day and the hour of thy departure."

Father Bishop noted the number of times that the letter "X" appeared within Robbie's writings. "This was written four times on this first occasion and was repeated several times during the exorcism, usually in answer to the question, *diem* day ."

Robbie also repeated, with a slight change, a line that his cousin had written down for him at the beginning of the night's events. "I will stay 10 days and then return after the 4 days are up." Such a statement would only make sense if the demon had returned on Wednesday. If Friday, March 25 had been the tenth day and the demon had remained absent on Saturday, Sunday, Monday and Tuesday, the writings made sense. However, Robbie had not shown any signs of the possession on Wednesday night and the demon had not manifested again until Thursday. There are some who believe, perhaps in an effort to make the statement correct, that Robbie could have started showing signs of the possession on Wednesday but Father Bowdern was not there to assess his condition. For this reason, the possession went unnoticed until Thursday, when the symptoms peaked once more. If this is the case, then the words that Robbie wrote become eerily accurate.

During the exorcism, the commands of the priest go beyond simply a demand for the time of the demon's departure. The demon is also commanded to reveal his name and speak in Latin. At one point during the night, the response came

112

in incomprehensible marks on the paper. The marks were not letters of the standard alphabet. Another response was very specific, though. It read: "I speak the language ﬄithe word "language" was misspelledﬄ of the persons. I will put in ﬄRobbie's real nameﬄ mind when he makes up his mind that the priests ﬄalso misspelledﬄ are wrong about writing English. I will, that is the devil will try to get his mother and dad to hate the Catholic Church. I will answer to the name of Spite."

Another statement in response to the command read: "I am the devil himself." This was followed by an odd sentence that read: "You will have to pray for a month in the Catholic Church." There was no indication as to "you" might be and whether "for a month" literally meant praying for a month or that the demon would stay with Robbie for a month. None of the Jesuits were able to figure out just what this remark meant.

Most of the other writings and drawings from this chaotic night were just as confusing. Few of them made any sense whatsoever. One of the drawings stunned Father Bishop however. It was of a human face. It was too badly drawn to recognize it but next to it were two words: "dead bishop."

It was another line that did not bode well for Robbie, though. The line stated: "You may not believe me. Then ﬄRobbie's real nameﬄ will suffer forever."

Robbie had been learning about Catholicism since the day that he had been taken to the St. Francis Xavier rectory. After relapsing into possession, Father Bowdern began working hard to get Robbie into the Catholic Church. He believed, as he did when he began the boy's instruction, that his entry into the Church would help him to battle the dark forces that were being confronted. Today, the conversion of a Protestant to Catholicism usually does not require baptism, especially since most Protestants especially Lutherans have already been baptized. The Church normally considers baptisms by other churches as valid. But prior to the reforms of Vatican II in the 1960s, conditional baptism, which was performed in case the Protestant baptism had not been valid for some reason, was more common than it is today. Father Bowdern did not want to take any chances. On his recommendation, Robbie and his parents agreed that the boy should be baptized as a Catholic. This would be followed by instruction in the next two sacraments of confession and Holy Communion.

The date for the baptism was set for Friday, April 1, at St. Francis Xavier Church. Father Bowdern picked the time so that it would occur before Robbie's usual spells began in the evening.

Robbie and his family left for the church around 7:30 p.m. Robbie was sitting in the back seat of the car between his mother and father, who had returned from Maryland after receiving word that thing with Robbie had gotten bad again. Robbie's uncle was driving and was rounding a corner a few blocks from the church when his nephew suddenly sprang forward from the back seat, letting out an inhuman howl as he did so.

Just moments before, Robbie had complained to his mother that he was feeling sick. His parents assumed that it was nervousness about the baptism and spoke softly to try and calm the boy's fears. Just then, the car radio, which had been quietly playing music, began transmitting only static. A moment later, Robbie exploded with rage. "So you are going to baptize me!" he screamed in a horrible, guttural voice. Then, the jangling, repetitive laugh filled the car. He howled at them, "And you think you will drive me out with Holy Communion?" He screeched and continued to laugh as he flew across the seat at his uncle.

Robbie grabbed the steering wheel and spun it so that the automobile headed directly for the curb. "You son of a bitch!" he yelled at his uncle when the man fought to pull Robbie's hand off the wheel. Finally, his uncle reached down and pulled on the emergency brake. The car screeched to a stop, its front bumper resting against a light post.

Robbie let go of the wheel and then turned and grabbed his mother by the throat. His uncle turned the ignition of the car and shut it off but the radio continued to blare static. It crackled loudly as Robbie's howled and beat against his mother. Robbie's father grabbed his son by the shoulders and pulled him back. As he did so, his mother slipped out of the car and changed places with Robbie's uncle, who had climbed out and jumped into the backseat with Robbie and his father. The two men forced him down on the seat, with Robbie biting and barking at them, and his mother started the car again and continued to drive towards the church. Robbie's aunt switched off the radio, but according to her later recollections, it continued to transmit loud bursts of static.

As the car rolled to a stop on Lindell Boulevard, in front of the church, Robbie's uncle and father hauled the boy out of the backseat. Father Bowdern, who had been standing near the doors waiting for them to arrive, heard the sound of screaming and yelling and went out to see what was going on. As he ran outside, he saw Robbie being wrestled to the sidewalk by his father and uncle. Robbie was screaming, swinging his fists and kicking at them while his mother and aunt cowered in the car, too terrified to get out. After a few moments, the two men began dragging Robbie toward the church steps. He was spitting at them, cursing loudly and laughing that same maniacal laugh.

Father Bowdern, fearing desecration of the church, decided to keep Robbie from coming inside. He told the men to take him to the rectory instead. Father Bowdern hurried ahead of them to open the door and Robbie was taken inside. He continued to howl like a dog, scream incoherent words and vomit huge splatters of mucus and blood onto his father, his uncle and the priest. Father

Bowdern got a pitcher of ice water from the refrigerator in the kitchen and he threw into Robbie's red and contorted face.

The boy calmed for a moment and his father and uncle pulled him to his feet. He suddenly went limp and refused to walk. As he dangled between them, his head pitched back and he laughed loudly. The laughter was joined by curses and the men began dragging him up the stairs to the third floor room that he had earlier occupied. They threw him onto the bed and held down his arms and legs, waiting for Father Bowdern to arrive. He soon appeared, intent on continuing the baptism, even if it was not the formal ritual that had been planned.

"Do you renounce Satan and all his works"" Father Bowdern loudly demanded from the end of the bed.

Robbie snarled at him and lurched forward, nearly breaking the grasp of his father and uncle. He managed to spit several feet and the mucus splattered on the priest's face.

Father Bowdern repeated his query. "Do you renounce Satan and all his works?"

The boy reacted even more violently. His body arched upward and he again nearly managed to spring off the bed and attack Father Bowdern. Only a renewed effort by the two man managed to keep the boy flat on the mattress.

Father Bowdern asked the question a third time and then a fourth. This time, Robbie's eyes snapped open and for a moment, he was no violent hellion, just a tired and weakened young boy. "I do renounce Satan and all his works," he managed to whisper. Then, his eyes closed again and he tried once more to rip himself from the hands of the men holding him. He began spitting again and Father Bowdern was again showered with blood and mucus.

He refused to let this faze him, however, and he began to offer the sacrament of baptism. The first touch of holy water on the boy's face sent him into the worst rage of the night. He writhed, spat and cursed as Father Bowdern splashed him again and again. For an instant, he thought that he saw a glimpse of the real Robbie and he began to speak in Latin: "I baptize thee in the name of the Father..."

The words triggered another rage, which Father Bowdern responded to with another splash of holy water. By following each set of words with another splash of holy water, Father Bowdern completed the baptism. This took nearly four hours and when he was convinced that Robbie had finally been baptized, he began to recite the now familiar prayers of exorcism. The night of terror finally came to an end near 11:30 p.m.

After Robbie finally went into a real sleep, his uncle left with his wife and Robbie's mother. The two women were still badly shaken from the wild ride to the church. Robbie's father chose to stay at the rectory and spend another night on the couch near Robbie's bed.

Although Father Bishop had hoped that baptizing Robbie into the Catholic faith would strengthen the boy against demonic attacks, he was not completely prepared for what happened next. Instead of getting better, Robbie grew worse. He became even more violent and wilder than ever before. On Saturday, April 2, he woke from his normal sleep and for the first time, slipped into a horrific trance state that lasted for more than fifteen hours. Father Bishop wrote in the diary: "It was evident that a struggle was at hand."

The boy never left his bed that morning. He simply went from deep sleep to thrashing about incoherently, howling, barking and wailing in a voice so loud that it could be heard throughout the entire rectory. Before anyone could get close enough to Robbie and pin him down, he had hurled a pillow at an overhead light, which shattered the shade and bulb. He also broke a wash basin but no one was sure how he managed to do it since it was on the other side of the room.

After these dramatic hours passed, Father Bowdern realized that he had little time to wait. He decided to follow the baptism with Holy Communion on the following day. During a period of calm, he and his assistant pastor, Father Joseph McMahon, a kind and gentle man who had started to establish a good relationship with the boy, began preparing Robbie for his first communion. Part of the process involved an examination of the conscience, when Robbie was asked to look into his heart and seek forgiveness for any wrongdoings that he may have committed. Perhaps the worst things that he had ever done had been during the time that he was possessed, although he claimed to have no knowledge of them. This lack of knowledge about what happened during the trances made the possession seem even more authentic to the priests. It meant that the events that occurred never entered into Robbie's consciousness.

Although Robbie was taught to examine his conscience in preparation for confession, he did not make his first confession on this day. The "exorcist's diary" moves from the fifteen hours of violence to the preparations for Holy Communion. Father Bowdern gave Robbie conditional absolution, forgiving him for any sins that he would have admitted to in the confessional. It was obvious that the Jesuits wanted to have Robbie receive his first communion as soon as possible.

To prepare Robbie, Father Bowdern called in Father Bishop and Father John G. O'Flaherty, S.J., a Jesuit from Kansas City. Father Bowdern had gotten to know Father O'Flaherty when he taught algebra, Latin and English at Campion High School. Although O'Flaherty had not been a great teacher, Father Bowdern knew that he would make a great parish priest. He understood people, preached

116

touching sermons that spoke to life experiences and had a quiet reverence about him that appealed to the average person. Father Bowdern also knew that his friend was a man who could be trusted and would not damage the veil of secrecy that hung over the exorcism.

Robbie remained motionless on the bed as Father Bowdern gave him conditional absolution. However, as he began the prayers for communion, the boy began to shift and twitch. Father Bishop and Father O'Flaherty moved to hold the boy down but, even though he moved about, he offered little resistance. Not expecting too much trouble, Father Bowdern stepped in close with the Communion host in his outstretched hand. One of the other priests held a linen cloth under the boy's chin so that the host would not be desecrated if it was not placed in his mouth.

As he came closer, Robbie suddenly began to seize and jerk about on the bed. His arms and legs swung and kicked and he began to growl and bark with rage. Father Bowdern quickly placed the host in the boy's mouth but Robbie spit it out. It landed on the cloth and Father Bowdern tried again. Robbie coughed it out once more and over the course of the next two hours, he tried to give it to Robbie two more times. He was unsure of what to do next but Father O'Flaherty had a suggestion. As this was the first Saturday of the month, he knew that services for Our Lady of Fatima were held in many churches, including St. Francis Xavier. He suggested that they say a rosary in honor of the Our Lady of Fatima. When the three priests finished the rosary, Father Bowdern tried once more to place the host in Robbie's mouth. This time, he swallowed it. Robbie had made his first Holy Communion.

As soon as he did, the atmosphere in the room seemed to change. Robbie's eyes came open and he seemed calm and relaxed. The weird rage that he had been in just a few moments before had disappeared completely. Father Bowdern told him that he could get dressed and that he was going to drive to the house in Bel-Nor with his father.

While Robbie was getting dressed, Father O'Flaherty went downstairs to bring around the rectory car. The others soon followed and Father Bowdern and Robbie's father climbed into the backseat with the boy between them. Robbie was happy and smiling and the priests were chatting with the boy as they pulled away from the curb. As soon as they started down the street, Robbie unexpectedly let out a loud and prolonged growl and he flung himself forward and grabbed Father O'Flaherty by the neck. The two men in the backset quickly grabbed hold of the boy and pried his hands from the other man's neck, leaving dark, red welts behind. Robbie's father and the priest were forced to hold Robbie down for the remainder of the journey to the house.

When they reached Roanoke Drive, Robbie changed again. He told his mother that he was starving and he sat down to eat a large breakfast. His family watched him closely throughout the day. They stated that at one moment he would be walking about the house, looking for something to do, and the next, he would be crouched in a corner with his eyes half-closed, growling quietly under his breath.

Later that evening, Father Bowdern returned and brought Father Bishop and Father O'Flaherty with him. They also brought along another relic, a tiny splinter that was revered as being a piece of the True Cross, the wooden post that Jesus had been crucified on. The relic was enshrined in a small golden case, which Father Bowdern placed on a dresser that was out of Robbie's reach. At this point, I noticed that Walter Halloran had been missing from the "diary" for several days. In 2005, I asked him if he remembered why he missed the events that have been described in the preceding pages but he did not recall. He guessed that studies and other responsibilities must have kept them away. He did remember hearing about the sequence of events from Father Bowdern and Father Bishop after they occurred.

This would prove to be one of the strangest nights of the exorcism so far.

Robbie sat on his bed in his underwear while Father Bowdern began reciting the prayers of exorcism. At first, Robbie showed no response to the prayers. He seemed bored and distracted and at one point, asked his mother for a dish of ice cream. For some reason, Father Bowdern allowed him to have it and he sat on the bed and ate ice cream as the Jesuits continued to pray. Then suddenly, he jumped off the bed and ran downstairs. Fearing that the boy might turn violent, Father Bowdern followed him and ordered him to return to the bedroom. Robbie nodded and with his head down, as if in shame, he climbed the stairs back to the second floor with Father Bowdern right behind him. He walked very slowly, until he reached the top of the steps. At that point, he broke into a mad run, racing into the bedroom and searching for the relic box that had been left on the dresser. Robbie was fast but Father O'Flaherty was faster. He slapped the boy's hand away but Robbie managed to rip the copy of the *Rituale Romanum* away from him and tear out several pages before anyone could stop him.

When Father Bowdern came into the room, Robbie was squatting on the bed with the torn pages from the prayer book clutched in his hands. He was laughing manically with that same repetitive and maddening sound. Father Bowdern chose to ignore him. He opened another copy of the book and began to read in Latin. "Thou shalt tell me by some sign or other thy name and the day and the hour of thy departure," he commanded the demon and then started to read again.

118

Robbie interrupted him before he could continue, though, startling everyone in the room. "*Dicas mihi nomen tuum, diem....*" he started and then added a few words in English. "Stick it up your ass," he said.

The Latin words that Robbie spoke were the same ones that Father Bowdern had just spoken, commanding the demon to reveal his name. He repeated them perfectly and seemed to understand the meaning of them -- as if he had been asked to reveal his name and told the priest to "stick it up his ass" in reply. This incident has been debated by those who have studied this case over the years. Many have noted this incident as proof that Robbie was genuinely possessed, having used with apparent understanding a language that he had no knowledge of prior to that moment. Others have dismissed this as simply a boy who mimicked the language of the prayer and had no idea what the words meant. The fact that he repeated the words that Father Bowdern had just spoken adds some credibility to this dismissal. Even Walter Halloran would remark years later that Robbie often copied or echoed the Latin prayers and phrases used by the Jesuits. Father Halloran did not believe that the boy exhibited any sign of understanding what he was saying.

But -- if Robbie was genuinely possessed -- could the demon have not used just such a method to try and confuse the priests about the authenticity of the case? The *Rituale Romanum* often warned them not to engage in conversation with the possessed person because the spirit wanted nothing more than to cause confusion and disharmony among those who battled against it. What better way to cause confusion than to make the priests believe that Robbie could be faking the whole thing? If the Jesuits became disenchanted enough with the situation, they might be convinced to call off the exorcism, which would be exactly what the demon would want.

If this was the case, any confusion caused by Robbie's possible mimicry was lost on Father Bowdern. He was more convinced than ever that the possession was genuine and on this night, Robbie's use of Latin phrases made him more determined than ever to continue. He kept reading from the prayer book, again demanding that it reveal the time when it would depart. He was forced to raise his voice when he did so because it was almost impossible for him to be heard over the sound of Robbie screaming for him to "Shut up! Shut up!"

The reading of the exorcism prayers continued for the next four hours. Father Bowdern continued to read in Latin and Robbie sometimes echoed it or responded with that hideous laugh or simply cursed at the priest. But things soon took another turn as the markings on Robbie's body returned once again.

Father Bowdern happened to glance down at the boy and saw that three vividly red scratches, in parallel lines, had appeared on his leg. Slowly, another large and jagged "X" manifested on his skin and then more scratches appeared.

These last scratches, which oozed with bright, red blood, shifted to form the numbers "18." Soon, another "18" appeared and then another and another. The "exorcist's diary" does not state where the markings appeared on his body but since Robbie was wearing only his boxer shorts, they could have been anywhere.

Finally, 1:15 a.m., Robbie came out the trance and he weakly asked his father for permission to get out of the bed so that he could sit down in a chair. His father helped him up and the boy shakily crossed the floor and sat down. His hands were trembling and while he had been scared many times before, on this night he was absolutely terrified.

"Please take me home," he pleaded with his father, who was returning to Maryland and his work at the first of the week. "I can't stand it here. I'm going crazy."

The possession had taken another, perhaps even darker turn. Robbie had never come out of a trance with any awareness of what had been happening to him. On this night, he seemed to know that something was very, very wrong. He may -- or may not -- have known that he was possessed but he definitely believed that he was going insane.

Robbie began the next day, which was Sunday, April 3, in an almost identical manner as the day before. He stirred long enough to launch a pillow at the overhead ceiling light and then went back to sleep. He woke again a short time later, acting very confused, and then fell asleep again. He finally regained consciousness at about 11:30 a.m. but refused to leave his bed. His mother finally brought him breakfast in bed. After he ate, he went downstairs and wandered about, looking very pale and acting very withdrawn.

His father suggested a game of baseball in the yard. He recruited Robbie's uncles and his cousin for the game and they went outside and started tossing around the ball. Robbie played with little interest, his attention obviously somewhere else, but his father was convinced that his son was just tired and a couple of hours in the fresh air would bring him around. Robbie loved baseball and it was a beautiful spring day in St. Louis. He also knew that the boy was happy at the fact that he was returning to Maryland soon, leaving all of the bad memories behind them.

One of Robbie's uncles tossed him the baseball but Robbie simply stood there, looking at it as though he had never seen anything like it before. He stood there for a moment and then his fingers opened and the ball fell to the ground with a soft thud. He staggered for a moment and then it was as if something had gripped him. Robbie began to run across the yard, straight past his father, who saw that the boy's eyes were tightly closed -- just as they were during one of his trances. He and the others dashed after Robbie, who began to run even faster as

120

he crossed into the neighbor's yard. He was sprinting away, eyes still squeezed shut, when his father finally grabbed him. Robbie broke away but his uncles quickly tackled him. The three men had to carry him home.

When they got him into the house, they sat him down at the kitchen table and his mother brought over a glass of water. He never noticed. His eyes were still closed and he shifted his body, stuck a leg under the table and lifted it off the floor. The water glass tipped over and spilled its contents onto the table top.

Robbie opened his eyes a few minutes later but it was almost like he was not in the room. He seemed to drift in and out of awareness, hanging in a state of eerie calm that was almost like a hypnotic trance. It was similar to a state of suspended animation or a drug-induced high. He swayed back and forth in his chair, never responding to anyone who addressed him. He never became violent, as he often did, but his family was still nervous about this new "lifeless" state. Robbie and his parents were supposed to be returning to Maryland the next day and they were worried about how he would act on the train. Not surprisingly, they put in a call to Father Bowdern and asked him to come back to the house on Roanoke Drive.

Father Bowdern arrived that night with Father Bishop, Father Van Roo and Father O'Flaherty. The priests gathered everyone in the living room so that they could talk to them and also so that they could observe Robbie, who had regained his consciousness but appeared weak and drained. He sat slumped in a chair, hardly able to keep his eyes open.

Suddenly, though, without any warning, Robbie sprang the chair and hurled himself across the room. He seized his aunt, reaching for her throat and managed to snag the collar of her dress instead. He jerked hard on the cloth and clawed at her, growling and snarling like an animal. Robbie's uncle was the first to react and he grabbed the boy around the waist. Robbie slipped away from him, his aunt's dress still gripped tightly in his hands, and he reached for her again. Robbie's father and all four of the priests pounced on the struggling boy, getting his aunt out of his reach and pinning him to the floor.

Robbie's uncle roughly shoved the priests out of the way and grabbed hold of Robbie and carried the boy upstairs. Angrily, he threw him onto the bed. His tolerance for Robbie's spells was at an end. This was the second time that the boy had acted his aunt and no matter how sick he might be, the uncle had reached the end of the limits of his endurance.

Just then, Robbie began to giggle and starting singing a little tune in a chilling, high-pitched voice. At first, his uncle was unable to understand what he was saying and then it became all too clear. Robbie was signing about his young cousin, a boy he had always been close with. He giggled and sang the boy's name several times and then, in that same eerie voice, began repeating: "You will die tonight. You will die tonight. You will die tonight...."

Someone -- and Father Bishop does not say who it was, but based on his earlier behavior, it was likely his uncle -- grabbed a pillow and pushed it down onto Robbie's face, muffling his song and threatening to smother the boy. Cooler heads soon prevailed and the pillow was pulled away. If nothing else, the violence had ended the boy's horrible singing and he lay there silent on the bed as Father Bowdern began the prayers of exorcism.

Over the course of the next two hours, he showed absolutely no emotion and made no sound. Finally, Robbie seemed to go into a natural sleep but he was restless, tossing and turning and snoring loudly. At midnight, the priests left and it was almost as if Robbie was waiting for them to depart. The members of his family were obviously the weakest of those he could choose to torment and with the Jesuits gone, he turned his attentions to them.

Moments after the priests drove away, Robbie exploded with violence. He became so vicious that his father and his uncle put gloves on his hands and then bound his hands and arms with heavy shipping tape. Robbie paused in his screaming and howling to whine about the pain caused by the tape and his father and uncle relented and decide to remove it. As soon as they did, though, he laughed at their gullibility and flew into another rage. The two men grappled and struggled with Robbie until he finally fell asleep at 3:30 a.m. on Monday morning.

When Father Bowdern heard about Robbie's antics following his departure the night before, he decided to accompany the family back to Maryland on the 9:50 a.m. train. He asked Father Van Roo to join him on the journey and for Father O'Flaherty to fill in for him at St. Francis Xavier. It was a serious and impulsive decision but Father Bowdern had almost complete autonomy over the case and he did not need the approval of his superiors to make the trip. He and Father Van Roo packed overnight bags and prepared to meet Robbie's family at the train station.

At the house on Roanoke Drive, preparations for the journey were not going as smoothly. Robbie simply refused to wake up. It was not until he was doused repeatedly with cold water that he finally could be pulled from bed and dressed. His father had to carry him to his uncle's car so that they could drive to the train station. Surprisingly, especially after other recent journeys in the automobile, the trip to the station was peaceful and by the time that they were ready to board the train, Robbie was happy and smiling and seemed to be his old self again.

For the most part, the journey to Maryland went smoothly. The Jesuits stayed in one compartment on the train and Robbie's family stayed in another.

122

During the day, Robbie was completely at ease, reading, playing games and watching the scenery go by. Father Van Roo spent most of his time reading and Father Bowdern began making preparations for Holy Week, the busiest time of the church year. He worked on his sermons and plans as much as he could, knowing that the trip to Maryland would have to be a short one so that he could get back to his church for this hectic time.

Around 11:30 p.m., when everyone was settled for the night, Father Bowdern heard a porter running down the aisle toward Robbie's family's compartment. Soon, another porter hurried past. Concerned, Father Bowdern and Father Van Roo followed. When they arrived, the found Robbie and his parents in their nightclothes and robes. The boy was acting very erratic and was unable to calm down. He fidgeted and spoke loudly, talking non-stop to the porters. Robbie's father explained to the priests that Robbie kept pressing the service button.

Father Bowdern left the compartment and took one of the porters aside. He told the man that the staff should ignore any further service calls from that compartment. The porter, sensing something that went beyond mere mischief, asked the priest what was wrong with the boy. Father Bowdern told him that the boy was just "high strung."

Robbie eventually went to sleep and woke up well before the train arrived in Washington on Tuesday, April 5. He seemed happy to be home and his parents wondered again if perhaps whatever was ailing him had been left behind in the other city.

Father Bowdern and Father Van Roo checked into a local hotel and Father Bowdern began making plans to try and get Robbie some assistance in Maryland. The Jesuit was the pastor of a large parish in St. Louis, he explained to officials that he met with, and needed to get home as soon as possible for Holy Week. However, he would remain in the Washington area until someone could be appointed to continue the case.

There is no record of the meetings that occurred while Father Bowdern was in Maryland and in the Washington area. According to reports, he was supposed to have met with a number of officials, who would do nothing with Robbie's case other than allow Father Bowdern to continue the exorcism while he was there. This was not Father Bowdern's intention, however. Because of Robbie's growing inclination toward violence, he wanted to see the boy confined and restrained, preferably in a Catholic mental institution before the exorcism was continued. He had no luck with this, however. No one wanted any part of the situation. He visited a number of different hospitals and even a mental institution operated by nuns in Baltimore. The nuns told Father Bowdern that they would take Robbie in, but the doctors at the institution objected. If Robbie was admitted as a psychiatric patient, they would agree, but they could not afford the ridicule and possible financial loss associated with an exorcism. The state of Maryland subsidized much of their patient care and for this reason, no one in an official capacity could learn of a "possessed boy" being admitted to the facility.

Disappointed, Father Bowdern made one last telephone call. As a worst case scenario, he called the Alexian Brothers Hospital in St. Louis and he was assured by Brother Rector Cornelius that Robbie could be placed there if necessary. Father Bowdern thanked him but kept trying to find a place for the boy in Maryland.

While this was taking place, Robbie was trying to adjust to being home again. Because he had missed so much school, his parents had decided to hold him back until the fall. This left him plenty of time to stay home, do chores and enjoy the warm spring weather. He spent most of one day working on a small garden plot in the backyard and cutting the lawn. He seemed to be enjoying himself and when bedtime came that night, he seemed contented and sleepy.

Robbie went to bed around 8:30 p.m. and for a time, all was quiet from the second floor. Then, his parents and his grandmother began to hear the sounds of something stirring upstairs. The noises were faint at first, a quiet thumping, but then Robbie cried out. It was happening again.

Father Bowdern and Father Van Roo arrived a half hour later and found Robbie shaking in his bed. Without hesitation, Father Bowdern began to read from the prayers of exorcism. He had barely begun to read when Robbie began to thrash about on the bed and he ripped open his pajama shirt. On the skin of his chest was a large scratch that was tearing across his skin as the two priests watched. Suddenly, two more scratches opened up and appeared on his chest. Author Thomas Allen described it as "if the blade of a razor was moving inside of his skin." Robbie screamed in pain and the priests realized that the marks on his body had created a numeral "4".

Father Bowdern continued with the ritual and at the word "*Jesu*", Robbie cried out again and told everyone who was present, including his family, to look at his legs. His mother pulled away the sheet and removed his pajama pants to show more of the mysterious marks. These new scratches were bright red and oozing blood. There were two of them and they were deep lines that ran down each of his legs from his thigh to his ankle.

More marks appeared as Father Bowdern went on with the prayers. Each time that he mentioned the names of "Jesus" or "Mary," Robbie winced with pain. Red marks appeared, scratches creased his skin and then, the words began to appear once again. When Father Bowdern asked for the name and the departure day of the demon, the reply came as bloody scratches in the boy's flesh. The words "hell" and "spite" appeared, as well as a series of numbers, which were imprinted on his skin: "4, 8, 10, 16."

124

As Robbie continued to squirm on the bed, hissing with pain, a strange, dark voice issued from his mouth. The priests had heard it before during the course of the exorcism and Robbie's parents swore that it was not a voice they had ever heard before. "I will not go," the voice croaked at them, "until a certain word is pronounced and this boy will never say it."

After Father Bowdern finished the third major prayer in the ritual, he and Father Van Roo carefully examined Robbie's body, looking at his stomach, chest and legs. They counted at least twenty different sets of scratches. Some of them were single marks but others were two or four side-by-side creases that were made at the same time. Robbie's hands had been in sight during the entire prayer session and both priests even the more skeptical Father Van Roo agreed that he could not have made the scratches with his own hands. At the same time the priests were studying the marks, Robbie moaned again and the two Jesuits saw another mark moving slowly down his leg.

Robbie suddenly began cursing, howling and spitting. Mucus, saliva and blood spattered the faces of both priests -- drenching amounts of liquid that perplexed Father Van Roo. He estimated that the boy was able to spit as much as a half pint of liquid in a matter of minutes. It was enough so that the faces of both men were soaking and so that Father Bowdern's glasses were so crusted that he was barely able to see. Father Van Roo was sometimes forced to wipe off the glasses with a towel and hold them in front of Father Bowdern so that he could continue to read.

Robbie, who had been hitting his targets without ever opening his eyes, stopped spitting and began to sing in a cackling high-pitched voice. He sang dirty songs and added to them with further obscenities and blasphemies that were not recorded in the "exorcist's diary." As he continued, he sang faster and faster, twitched and contorted with more anger and seemed almost to thrum with activity. Father Bowdern continued to read, believing that the boy was building toward some sort of breaking point.

Robbie's right hand began to move on his chest. For the first time, the boy began creating the scratches on his own skin. As his fingers moved, his nails became soaked with blood. He was scratching two words on his bony chest in large, capital letters. The words spelled "HELL" and "CHRIST." Father Van Roo pulled the boy's hands away from his body and held them down on the bed. Meanwhile, Robbie chortled his high, keening laugh and continued singing.

Exhausted, Father Bowdern looked over at the clock on the nightstand. It was nearly 2:00 a.m. As soon as he turned his head, Robbie growled at him. "I'll keep you 'til 6," he said in the same deep voice that had come from his throat earlier. "To prove it, I'll put him to sleep and then wake him up."

125

The words left his lips and then instantly, Robbie went from his thrashing spell to a deep sleep. The priests tried several times to awaken him but he refused to come around. Father Van Roo even went as far as to pinch him on the arm but the boy never flinched. He was now in a state of sleep so complete that it was unnatural. Then, fifteen minutes later, Robbie was startled awake. He was so frightened that he was shaking but he was unable to express just what it was that was bothering him. Father Bowdern steeled himself for another four hours of terror, as the demon had predicted, but it never occurred. A few moments later, Robbie fell back to sleep again and the night was over.

The Jesuits slowly descended the stairs and said good night to the family. They went back to their hotel, two troubled and worried men. Robbie was not getting any better and Father Bowdern had still not found anywhere in the area that would take him in. He was beginning to fear that he would have to return Robbie to St. Louis.

The next day, Friday, Father Bowdern prayed for the strength to continue. He knew that he had to get Robbie into a place where he could be restrained. He never stopped believing that the possession would pass but he also believed that things were going to get much worse before they got better. After another fruitless day of searching for a place to place Robbie in Maryland, Father Bowdern sat down with the boy's parents and convinced them to return to St. Louis and allow him to continue the exorcism at the Alexian Brothers Hospital. Father Van Roo arranged for a return trip by train and he called the Alexians to let them know that Robbie would be arriving at the hospital on Sunday, April 10. It was Palm Sunday, the beginning of Holy Week.

The priests had dinner with the family that evening and at about 8:00 p.m., Robbie went into the bathroom to brush his teeth. A few minutes later, everyone in the house heard cursing and screaming coming from the bathroom. His mother ran in to see what was going on and immediately called for Father Bowdern. As he hurried in, the boy was hurling spit from his mouth and howling obscenities. Father Bowdern later told Father Bishop that he had never seen the boy act so diabolical and that his words were so foul that he refused to say them aloud so that they could be recorded in the "diary." Father Bishop only wrote of the night that "there was filthy talk and movements and filthy attacks on those at the bedside concerning masturbation and contraceptives, sexual relations of priests and nuns."

For three hours, Father Bowdern and Father Van Roo prayed while Robbie spattered the priests with mucus and spit and jerked his hand up and down as an imitation of masturbation. He tore at the priest's clothing, threw pillows, tore the sheets, sang in the high-pitched warble and acted as if he were responding

126

to the Latin phrases of the prayer with jumbled Latin phrases of his own. When he spoke, he did so in the deep, rumbling voice that was becoming familiar to the Jesuits.

Father Bowdern had hoped to administer Holy Communion to the boy on that night but Robbie was too frantic and wild for him to be able to do so. During a brief moment of calm, he tried to give Robbie a mild sedative but he spit it out. No sooner had he done so, though, Robbie grabbed the pill from the sheets and swallowed it. Within a few minutes, it began to work and soon he drifted off into a normal sleep.

On Saturday morning, Father Bowdern, Father Van Roo, Robbie and his mother boarded a train that was bound for St. Louis. The diary reported that: "R was normal all day. He underwent a short spell upon retiring in the evening."

By this point in the possession, the "exorcist's diary" was only providing details of events that were different from those already recorded. The continued urinating, the horrific smells, curses and obscenities had become part of the routine and were rarely noted in the diary's pages. Father Bishop also left out what the gravelly voice that came from Robbie said about the priests and assistants themselves. Walter Halloran told me that Robbie seemed to be very sensitive to the insecurities of everyone present, from the priests to Halloran and even Robbie's mother or father. He constantly tried to foster distrust among all of them.

"I don't know how he could have known some of the things that he said to us," Father Halloran recalled, "whether he overheard things, sensed them or perhaps had a way of knowing them that we can't explain but he came up with some pretty embarrassing stuff. None of it was ever recorded and I wouldn't want to bring any of them back up again."

Also unrecorded was the habit that Father Bowdern developed to hammer away at the demon. Father Halloran later remembered that he would stop his prayers in Latin and translate two of the phrases from the prayers into English. He would order the demon to state his name, then would pause for a response. Robbie would usually reply with more spitting and cursing. After that, Father Bowdern demanded the demon to reveal the day and hour that he would leave the boy. After that, Robbie became even more violent.

Father Bowdern had explained to Halloran that the exorcist was supposed to take note of the prayers or phrases that seemed to have the most effect on the demon and use them with greater stress and frequency. Since Robbie became so angry when asked these questions, he knew that he had found a weak spot. With this in mind, he asked the questions over and over again, tormenting the spirit that had taken control of the boy. He hoped that the demon was so angry because it knew that its time was near.

127

He prayed often that this was the case.

On Palm Sunday, Robbie returned to St. Louis and to the Alexian Brothers Hospital. He was taken to the same fifth floor security room in the old wing where he recently spent a single night. This time, he seemed unconcerned, it was recalled, about being housed on the mental ward but perhaps the kind words and manner of the Brothers who greeted him set the boy at ease. Brother Rector Cornelius, the monk in charge of the hospital, arranged for constant prayers for Robbie. A golden container containing a consecrated host was placed between two lighted candles in the chapel. During both day and night, monks filed in and out of the chapel to kneel and pray for him -- who they only knew as "the boy on the fifth floor."

The exorcism was officially a secret but the Brothers at prayer knew what was going on, as did many of the laymen on the hospital staff. Years later, many of them spoke of the strange sounds, smells and noises that emanated from the security room and even the entire fifth floor itself.

While Robbie was getting settled in the hospital, Father Bowdern was conducting Palm Sunday mass at St. Francis Xavier. The tired priest had many responsibilities that had to be handled, in addition to his continuing the exorcism. There were times when he wondered if he was capable of going on. His brother, Dr. Edward H. Bowdern, later stated that Father Bowdern "looked terrible." As a physician, he noticed things that most people would not, such as how much weight he had lost, the swelling around his eyes that he had never noticed before and, most shocking, the boils that had appeared on the priest's arms. He insisted that he be able to examine his brother thoroughly but Father Bowdern dismissed his concerns. It would not be until many years later that Dr. Bowdern would discover why his brother had been so sick and weak in 1949. Father Bowdern, keeping his vow of secrecy, never even told anyone in his family about the exorcism.

Around 7:00 p.m. on that Sunday evening, Father Bowdern was accompanied by Father Van Roo, Father O'Flaherty and Father Bishop to Robbie's hospital room. He spoke with Robbie for a little while and noticed that the boy seemed untroubled and calm. He had been reading quietly when the priests had entered the room. Father Bowdern decided that he would start the exorcism prayers right away, instead of waiting for a spell to begin, in hopes that it might have greater effect. The exorcism produced no response from Robbie and neither did the rosary that Father Bowdern recited. In fact, the boy even joined in. Together, they recited the prayer until nearly 11:00 p.m., when Robbie drifted off to sleep.

Father Bowdern waited for a few minutes and then shook Robbie awake to give him Holy Communion. The boy tried valiantly to take the host but could only stay awake for a few moments at a time. After several attempts to keep him conscious, Father Bowdern began to abandon the idea and then Robbie woke up suddenly and accepted communion. He lay back in his bed with a smile on his face and went to sleep again.

Palm Sunday had passed in peace and Bowdern began to hope that the power of Holy Week was helping to force the demon out of the boy once and for all.

On Monday morning, one of the brothers on the ward instructed Robbie to clean his room and then brought him along as the monk made his rounds throughout the ward. This became a routine for Robbie as he helped with odd jobs and then spent some time working, under one of the Brother's supervision, and studying his catechism. Father Bowdern had wanted Robbie's instruction in the Catholic faith to continue and he could not have found a better place for it - - nor a better group of men to continue it.

The hospital was a quiet place and a prayerful one. Every room had a crucifix on the wall and in the morning and in the evening, loudspeakers broadcast prayers led by the chaplain throughout the building. The Alexian Brothers were a kind, cheerful and essentially tireless group. They combined their intense personal faith with a commitment to provide care and compassion for their patients. The monks did not read newspapers and did not speak at meals, which were eaten at an assigned seat in the dining hall. When a monk died, a crucifix was placed on his chair every day for a week. Each of them worked for about eight hours each day and spent about another eight hours in prayer and meditation. They refrained from idle conversation, never walked outside alone and never visited one another in their private rooms. They began each day before sunrise and spent nearly an hour in prayer before doing anything else. The monks were usually in bed each night by 9:00 p.m.

In order to accommodate their religious schedule, the monks hired laymen, staff workers and nurses to work in the hospital. Many of them were recruited as young people from a local orphanage and all of them were trained by the Alexians. All of the staff members and nurses were men.

The devotion shown by the Alexian Brothers to their religion did not interfere with their medical training and objectivity, though. According to local legend in other words, not in the "diary" and not recalled by any of the principles in the case , Brother Rector Cornelius was said to have called in a non-Catholic pediatrician to have a look at Robbie. The doctor was allegedly sworn to secrecy and then asked to examine Robbie and provide the Alexian with any natural explanation for his condition. The pediatrician looked at Robbie's strange cuts, watched his sudden mood shifts, convulsions, weird spells and supposedly even saw objects move about the room in his presence. He reported back to Brother

Rector Cornelius, and legend has it that he stated quiet sincerely, "I can't give you a natural explanation for this."

On Monday evening, Father Bowdern, Father van Roo, Father Bishop and Walter Halloran entered Robbie's room. They brought with them some books, magazines and some Catholic readers to keep Robbie busy. The small group chatted for awhile and then Father Bowdern began the exorcism prayers again. Once more, they went uninterrupted.

Relieved, Father Bowdern closed the *Rituale Romanum* and took his rosary beads from his pocket. They had hardly started reciting the rosary when Robbie suddenly screamed and clutched at his chest. One of the priests leaned over and opened the boy's hospital gown and saw that dark red blood was seeping through it. Father Bowdern refused to be dissuaded from the prayers but as soon as he began reciting the rosary again, Robbie again began to scream. He tore open his clothing and large capital letters that spelled out "EXIT" appeared on his body. Moments later, a long scratch in the shape of an arrow materialized. It pointed down his chest in the direction of his groin. The same word appeared in three different places on Robbie's body that night.

Walter Halloran remembered the incident decades later: "I saw those marks appear on his skin. There was no way that he could have done it with his fingernails, not with us watching him. They were very red and sometimes bloody. And they just appeared there. I remember looking at him at one point and there was nothing. The next time I looked, there they were."

Robbie screamed again but this time it was because of the scratches. He said that the pain was coming from inside his body, motioning to the area around his kidneys. Then he said that his penis was burning and he began to urinate in a wild stream. Robbie wept, saying that it was hurting him very badly.

Father Bowdern hated to see the boy in pain but the urination actually gave him great hope. In many historical cases, demons had exited from their victims using urination or defecation and Father Bowdern hoped Robbie's case would be the same. He decided that he would strengthen Robbie's resolve by offering him Holy Communion.

At the mere mention of communion, though, Robbie began to bark, howl and scream. Several Alexians in the room held him down and quickly restrained him to the bed with leather straps. Robbie arched and strained against the bonds and his gown fell open to reveal more scratches and marks that were appearing on his body. The word "hell" appeared on his chest and then on his thigh. As Father Bowdern prayed, Robbie's body thrashed about and more scratches manifested on his skin.

Father Bowdern realized that Robbie reacted with the most violence whenever he spoke of "Holy Communion" or "Blessed Sacrament." He raised his voice to a shout, bellowing that he was giving Robbie communion, and leaned down close to the boy's contorted face. As he did so, Robbie's hand slipped out of the restraints and he punched the priest squarely in the testicles.

The boy let out a loud cackling laugh. "How'd you like that for a nutcracker?" he chortled and the priest staggered back to regain both his breath and his composure. The Alexians tightened the restraints and Robbie continued to slam and arch against them.

From his violent efforts came another of the great legends of the 1949 Exorcism. According to the stories, Robbie's body thrashed and contorted into seemingly impossible shapes. It was even said that he was able to curve his body backward on the bed until his head actually touched the back of his feet, creating a perfect bow. Reports from historic exorcisms often spoke of such things but Father Bishop's "diary" never mentioned it.

I asked Father Halloran if anything like this ever occurred during Robbie's stay at the hospital and he told me that it did not. "I never saw anything like that," he told me. "I have had other people ask me about that too but he never managed anything of that sort."

"Do you know how this story could have gotten started?" I asked.

Father Halloran surmised: "I would guess that one of the brothers may have told about how the boy strained and pulled at the restraints. That could be a little scary, I'll admit. The story probably got more dramatic as it was told over and over again."

After Father Bowdern recovered, he began to speak with more agitation about communion, speaking of the Last Supper, where, just before he was crucified, Jesus instituted the sacrament of Holy Communion. Father Bishop wrote that as Father Bowdern spoke, "scratches appeared from R's hips to his ankles in heavy lines, seeming as a protest to Holy Communion."

Father Bowdern had retrieved the consecrated host he had placed it out of reach to keep Robbie from desecrating it and returned to the bedside. Robbie, his eyes still pinched shut, turned his face toward Bowdern. A voice that Father Bishop identified as "the Devil's" spoke and uttered, "I will not allow him to receive."

Father Bowdern tried several times to place the host into Robbie's mouth but each attempt was greeted by thrashing, biting, barking and howling. The priest finally gave up and replaced the host in the small box that he had carried it in. He then decided to bestow Spiritual Communion on the boy instead. He explained that Robbie had only to want Jesus in communion and miraculously, Jesus would come to him.

Robbie began to speak, pausing and faltering as if it were nearly impossible for him to get the words out. "I want.... I want to receive.... you in Holy......"

Before he could say "Communion," though, a wave of anger and pain washed over him. He screamed and began to curse, terrifying the Alexians, who had never witnessed anything like it before. It was said that the entire ward -- including the staff, nurses and patients -- clearly heard the screams. The staff on the mental ward had certainly heard chilling screams before but they had never heard anything quite like this.

And then it was over. Robbie collapsed and plunged into a sleep of exhaustion. He did not awaken. Father Bowdern knocked weakly on the door for it to be opened and all of the weary men stumbled out into the corridor. Father Bishop was so tired that he did not even make a note as to the time the exorcism ended on this night.

On Tuesday night, the priests, the Alexians and Walter Halloran returned to Robbie's room. The boy had spent another uneventful day. At night, he could fill grown men with terror but each morning, he would appear to be quite normal and would profess to have no memory of the events that took place after dark. He usually spent the day reading comics, doing odd jobs with Alexians on the ward or playing board games with nursing students who filled in as assistants. When the men returned that evening, Robbie had already slipped into one of his trances. As they came into the room, they saw him lying there on the bed with his eyes closed. His body was twitching and jerking and he was obviously no longer the boy who spent peaceful days on the ward.

Father Bowdern knelt down at the side of the bed and quickly went through the Litany of Saints and the Our Father prayer, then recited the Fifty-Third Psalm. He soon began the litany of prayers that made up the exorcism ritual, waiting for responses from the others in the room. Now, the voices of the Jesuits were joined the Alexians, who stood by to help in whatever way they were needed. As Father Bowdern started the first prayer that summoned the evil spirit, Robbie began arching his back, straining his body and screaming and groaning in anticipation.

Father Bowdern began to read and when he got to the first command, he switched to English as he had been doing since he learned that it seemed to particularly aggravate the spirit inside of Robbie. He spoke: "Thou shalt tell me by some sign or other thy name and the day and the hour of thy departure. I command....."

"Stick it up your ass!" Robbie shouted from the bed and then he began to laugh in that creepy, high-pitched chortle.

132

The laughter broke off, though, and the voice abruptly changed to the deep-throated rumble that had been sending chills down the backs of the listeners. "I am the devil," the voice growled. "I will make him awaken and he will be pleasant. You will like him."

Robbie suddenly snapped open his eyes, smiled and looked around. He appeared to the boy that the Jesuits had come to like, who the Alexians had taken under their wing, who they had all read stories with, played games and laughed. But he did not remain with them for long. In a moment, his eyes closed and his body filled with tension again.

The deep, rattling voice returned. "I am the devil," it said this time, "and I will wake him up and he will be awful."

Robbie woke up again but this time he was angry and annoyed with the men who were holding onto him. He did not seem to be under the spell of the demon this time but he was more like the young boy they had also encountered in the past, the whining and irritable boy who wanted to have things his way and who didn't want to do his chores or school work.

He continued to grumble as the exorcism continued but the demon seemed to have left him. As the prayers ended, Father Bowdern began to recite the rosary, carefully watching Robbie as he did so. No scratches or marks appeared on him this night but the spirit was still making its influence known. When Father Bowdern attempted to give him Holy Communion again, the horrible voice came once again.

"I will not let Robbie receive Holy Communion!" it roared.

Moments later, the boy slipped into a deep but natural sleep and the Jesuits ended the session.

Father Bowdern sat for some time and meditated on the situation with Robbie. Things only seemed to change for the worse, but one thing remained consistent in that the boy continued to be stable during the day. There had been some minor incidents like the baseball game at his uncle's house but for the most part, Father Bowdern did not feel that Robbie was being threatened during the morning or afternoon hours. His periods of terror mostly seemed to come at night. Because of this, he felt that Robbie would be closer to God in the morning, so on Wednesday, he asked the hospital chaplain, Father Seraphim Widman, to give Robbie Holy Communion. Father Widman happily agreed and also offered to help with Robbie's Catholic instruction as well.

Father Bowdern agreed, gaining an ally within the hospital. Since Alexian brothers were not priests, they had to recruit chaplains from outside of their ranks. Father Widman came from a small religious order called the Missionaries of the Most Precious Blood and he had the unique position of being outside of the control of the archdiocese. This was necessary in order for him to be an objective evaluator of priests who were in the hospital suffering from alcohol or mental problems. He certified whether or not a priest who was undergoing treatment was spiritually capable of performing mass and even if the priest was ready for release or not. This made Father Widman "the priest who monitored other priests," a sort of "internal affairs" man for the archdiocese.

Being outside of the control of the authorities, Father Widman could have caused problems for Father Bowdern with the exorcism. The exorcism was taking place in a location that Father Widman controlled and it was being conducted in secret, thanks to orders from an archdiocese that Father Widman was not required to accept orders from. He could have presented a jurisdictional problem for the Jesuits, but he did not. Father Bowdern diplomatically made him a part of the exorcism by asking him to give Robbie communion and accepting his offer to instruct him in Catholicism. This insured that the two men would be able to work together -- no matter how long the exorcism might take.

Robbie received communion on that Wednesday morning and then was surprised when Jesuit scholastic Walter Halloran dropped by the hospital with an exciting offer. It was a warm spring day and he wanted to see if Robbie would be interested in taking a ride in the country. Robbie eagerly accepted.

The outing was a chance for Halloran to try and befriend the young boy. Even though Halloran knew that Robbie did not remember what occurred during the nighttime sessions, Halloran had often had to be almost brutal with the boy in order to subdue him and to keep him from hurting himself or someone else. Robbie may not have consciously remembered that Halloran had to do to him, but it was as though he somehow sensed the violence that occurred between them. Perhaps for this reason, Halloran felt that Robbie disliked him. This seemed to intensify Walter's feelings of guilt. He hoped that spending some time with Robbie would start to unthaw the chilliness between them.

Robbie was checked out of the hospital and into the custody of Walter Halloran and another Jesuit scholastic, Barney Hasbrook. Halloran drove them to White House, a Jesuit estate that stretched for about seventy-five acres along the bluffs of the Mississippi River. The estate was used as a Jesuit retreat center and had a long history in the region. Father Jacques Marquette, the Jesuit explorer and missionary, had first passed the spot when he came down the river in 1673 and the mansion had received its name of "White House" from a post-Civil War lobbying effort to move the nation's capital to St. Louis. The property was chosen by promoters to be the site of the new White House. The land was purchased by the Jesuits in 1922 and they established the St. Louis House of Retreats.

The White House, Jesuit Retreat, located west of St. Louis

Hasbrook drove and Halloran and Robbie sat in the back seat of the car as they made the trip south of the city and along the Mississippi River. When they arrived, Robbie seemed thrilled to be out in the fresh air and sunshine but only mildly interested in the limestone retreat house and the chapel. The Jesuits showed Robbie the relics of North American martyrs that were enshrined in the walls of the chapel and then they walked across the lawn toward the bluff. The view of the river and the farms of Illinois on the other side of it could only distract Robbie for a few minutes. Halloran was wishing for a baseball bat and a couple of gloves when he remembered the Stations of the Cross that were located on a path along the bluff. There, large white statues commemorated the last hours of Jesus as he carried the cross through the streets of Jerusalem to his place of execution. He asked Robbie if he would like to see the path, after explaining to him what it was, and Robbie quickly agreed.

Halloran led the way to the first station and told the story of it to Robbie. Robbie genuflected awkwardly but Halloran praised him for it. He explained that Catholics would walk from station to station, genuflecting at each one and then pausing for a moment to think about what had happened on the way of the cross. Robbie was intensely interested and eagerly asked about the next one. The three of them continued walking.

There was fourteen Stations of the Cross and Halloran began leading Robbie along the path, explaining the story behind each of them. As they continued to walk, though, Halloran felt more and more anxious. The path ran very close to the edge of the bluff and he was worried what might happen if Robbie's violent and strange behavior returned.

Robbie's face started to change. Halloran could not pinpoint what it was at first but something was definitely wrong. He turned to his friend, Barney Hasbrook, and told him that they needed to leave. But Halloran had noticed too late that Robbie was no longer himself.

Just as they reached the eleventh Station, "Jesus is Nailed to the Cross," Robbie started to scream and run. He stumbled onto the lawn and launched himself toward the edge of the bluff that loomed over the river. Halloran sprinted toward him, tackled the boy and tried to subdue him. Robbie fought him like a wild animal and it was not until Hasbrook arrived that they were able to pin him to the ground. Halloran had never seen Robbie behave this way during the daytime and was unsure what to do.

He and Hasbrook half-dragged and half-carried the boy to the car and they threw him into the backseat. Halloran held Robbie down as Hasbrook started the car and pulled out onto the main road. He needed all of his strength, as Robbie was fighting wildly. He battled the ferocious boy but at one point, Robbie broke free and lunged over the seat for the steering wheel. Hasbrook knocked his hands away and managed to keep them on the road until they got back to the hospital.

Several of the Alexians helped to get Robbie back to his room and assisted in calming him down. He soon came out of his spell and by the time that Father Bowdern arrived with the rest of the exorcism group around 9:00 p.m., the boy was smiling and happy. Father McMahon, the assistant pastor at St. Francis Xavier and Robbie's closest Jesuit friend, had given him some puzzle gadgets to play with and Robbie told the priest how much had liked them. Father Bowdern, although disturbed by Halloran's report from White House, took Robbie's calmness as a good sign and told everyone that it was time to begin. Robbie lay back on the bed and Halloran, Father McMahon and Father Bishop knelt around it. An Alexian on duty remained nearby. Father Bowdern then knelt too and he began the Litany of the Saints.

Robbie immediately went into one of his now legendary rages. Halloran seized hold of him and the nearby Alexian moved quickly to help. Two other monks, stationed outside, hurriedly unlocked the door and rushed to the bed. Robbie seemed to calm a little under their restraint and he opened his mouth to speak. Once again, several of those in the room claimed that the voice did not belong to the young boy. The deep, hoarse voice said: "God has told me to leave at 11 tonight ..... But not without a struggle."

According to Father Bishop, Robbie then reacted with more violence than he had seen at any other time in the exorcism. For the next twenty minutes, he jerked and thrashed, arching his body against the restraints and striking at his captors with his hands, nails and teeth. The screams could be heard all over the

136

hospital wing as Robbie howled, barked, cursed and screeched. Several of the Alexians were forced to leave the room and patrol the rest of the ward. When a patient began to react wildly, this behavior spread through the rest of the ward like a contagion. Reports say that during Robbie's outbursts, some of the most violent patients in the wing had to be restrained.

Meanwhile, Father Bowdern continued with the prayers, often drowned out by the sound of Robbie's fit. When the time came, he translated the usual passage from Latin to English and demanded to know when the demon would depart. The response came in what is now referred to as "Pig Latin" and was translated to mean "Stick it up your ass!" Robbie mocked the Latin passages of the prayer and then began to sing, in a grating falsetto voice, about sticking "it" up "your ass."

Father Bowdern ignored it and never wavered. He finished the prayers and began to recite the rosary. All of the men present joined in and the comforting sounds of the prayers filled the room.

At fifteen minutes before the promised departure time of 11:00 p.m., a church bell tolled. Robbie laughed and began to imitate the sound of the bell. When 11:00 p.m. came, the bell fell silent as everyone waited for the end of the session to come. The group was filled with anticipation, waiting for the demon to leave in whatever manner such things occurred.

They waited but the moment never came. Instead, they were assaulted by Robbie's eerie laughed and another uncanny imitation of the church bell. The *Rituale Romanum* had warned them -- never trust the word of a devil.

The prayers continued and the Alexians kept reciting the rosary on one side of the room. The murmuring sound of their prayers washed over everyone, giving Father Bowdern even more courage and hope than the stubborn priest already possessed. His courage prompted him to try and give Robbie Holy Communion as the bell tolled again at midnight.

As Father Bowdern began the preparations, the deep voice once again came from Robbie's throat. "I will not permit it," the voice growled at him.

Father Bowdern tried to place the consecrated host into the boy's mouth many times but each attempt ended with failure. Robbie refused to open his mouth or when he did, he snapped at the priest with this teeth. Finally, Father Bowdern resorted to Spiritual Communion again and began to encourage Robbie just to say the words: "I want to receive you in Holy Communion."

The dark voice roared with laughter at the priest but Robbie somehow seemed to awaken. He struggled past whatever was holding him back and he began to force the words from his lips. "I want.... I want...." he tried to speak but he was unable to manage the word "communion."

The session was ended for the night when Robbie lapsed into a deep and normal sleep.

The next morning, which was Holy Thursday, Robbie met with Father Widman, who experienced no problems when he gave the boy Holy Communion. Later in the afternoon, Walter Halloran dropped by and he and Robbie sat and talked about what Holy Week was all about. Robbie was interested, so he began telling him about the meaning behind Holy Communion and the Last Supper.

While he was speaking, Robbie began to shift back and forth on the bed, shaking his legs up and down. Halloran asked him what was wrong.

"My legs hurt," Robbie replied.

Robbie was sitting on the edge of his bed and so Halloran lifted the legs of his pajamas to take a look at them. He soon found that the boy's entire body was covered with scratches, welts and marks. Robbie began to cry. "I wish this would stop," he moaned. "I can't stand this anymore."

Halloran suggested the two of them pray together and as they did, the pain went away and the welts ands marks started to fade. Walter Halloran would remember this incident years later. "I saw the marks fade away right before my eyes," he told me. "There was no easy way to explain this other than to believe that the power of prayer eased the boy's suffering."

And it may have also been the power of prayer that caused Holy Thursday night to pass as peacefully as it did. At the same time that Father Bowdern was arriving in Robbie's room that evening, Catholics all over St. Louis were going into churches to receive Holy Communion and to pray before the Blessed Sacrament. Father Bowdern's prayers and rosaries filled the small hospital room and Robbie accepted them in a state of calm and quiet.

Good Friday, the day commemorated by Catholics as a day of mourning and loss, came and passed, as did Holy Saturday. This day marked three days of peace in the room on the fifth floor and Father Bowdern felt that an end was in sight. He believed that the exorcism would be completed in triumph during Easter. At a few minutes after midnight on Sunday morning, Father Bowdern spoke with the Alexians and made arrangements for Robbie to be awakened early in the morning, given Holy Communion and taken to Mass in the hospital's chapel.

Early the next morning, around 6:30, Father Widman arrived at Robbie's room. Another Alexian, who was the nurse on duty, was waiting for him and Father Widman asked him to wake up Robbie and help him to get ready. The monk shook him gently but the boy's eyes didn't open. He shook him again, a little harder this time. Robbie stayed asleep. He shrugged toward Father Widman, who frowned and placed the communion supplies on the desk. The priest then went over to the bed and grabbed Robbie by the shoulders. He shook him vigorously and then slapped his face two times. The boy finally woke up but he was groggy and unhappy.

Father Widman removed the host from its box and then, holding it between the index finger and thumb of his right hand, he made the sign of the cross in front of Robbie's closed eyes. He ordered Robbie to sit up and then said a short prayer before he brought the host toward the young man's lips. The boy knew it was there but his mouth stayed closed. Father Widman insisted that he open his mouth but Robbie ignored him. The priest asked him three more times and finally, on the fourth attempt, he managed to get the host into Robbie's mouth. Father Widman said a short prayer and then left to attend to his many Easter duties, leaving Robbie and the nurse alone.

The nurse, who had been reading when Father Widman arrived, re-opened his prayer book and sat back down in a chair next to the bed. He didn't notice that Robbie had climbed out of bed until the book was ripped from his hands. According to the nurse's later account, he tried to grab Robbie but the boy got away from him. He tried to subdue him but Robbie jerked out of hands and spit a thick gob of spit and mucus into the nurse's face. Finally, he grabbed the boy by the arm.

Robbie spun around and words belched forth from his mouth in that deep, baritone voice that the priest's believed belonged to the demon. "I will not let him go to mass," the voice said to the nurse. "Everyone thinks it will be good for him."

The nurse called for help from the hallway and several other Alexians managed to subdue Robbie and they got him back into bed.

Later in the morning, at St. Francis Xavier, Father Bowdern received word that he was needed urgently at the hospital. He had just completed the first of his Easter masses and the call could not have come at a worst time. Something had happened, though, he was told, and they needed him to come.

Robbie was in the throes of one of his seizures, screaming, fighting and cursing, when Father Bowdern arrived. The boy quieted down almost as soon as the Jesuit arrived and Father Bowdern was able to leave an hour or so later. His hopes for an Easter triumph in the case had been dashed and it was almost as if he had been summoned to the hospital just so that he would realize that fact.

Later that afternoon, Robbie had recovered enough from the earlier incidents that some of the monks took him outside to play some baseball and to enjoy some sunshine and fresh air. He seemed relaxed and happier than any of them had ever seen him. As the sun started to go down, one of the brothers, who had let Robbie work odd jobs with him and had taken a particular liking to him, told Robbie that it was time to go inside. They entered the hospital through a basement door and started down a hallway to the elevator. Suddenly, without any warning, Robbie stopped, turned and then punched the Alexian in the face with his fist. The monk stumbled backwards but thanks to his long experience with handling mentally ill patients, he quickly recovered. He reached out with a practiced move that would allow him to pin Robbie's elbows behind him but the boy was too fast. He slammed his body into the monk and drove him into the wall. The Alexian had no choice but to call for help.

Several other monks came running but by the time they reached their fallen comrade, he had been beaten and battered. Unable to believe that a small boy could inflict such damage, one of the monks stepped in to grab Robbie's arm. He received a solid punch in the face for his efforts, driving him back to the floor. Three other monks pushed their way toward the boy and began wrestling with him.

Robbie kicked, punched, scratched and bit at the monks. He kept screaming that he would kill them, over and over again. Finally, they managed to get him down, pin his arms and legs and carry him into an elevator and back to his room. It took six of them to strap Robbie down in his bed.

Father Bowdern was summoned back to the hospital again. When he came into the room, he again found Robbie in the midst of one of his fits. The boy was screaming and howling and throwing his body against the restraints. He seemed completely out of his mind but Father Bowdern knew that the horror inside of Robbie had nothing to do with mental illness. He said nothing to anyone else in the room. He simply opened his prayer book and began reading the exorcism ritual.

As the prayers went on, the deep, hoarse voice returned again. It shouted at them: "I will have ffiRobbie's real nameffl awaken and ask for a knife."

This could not have been good news to anyone, thanks to the death threats that Robbie had made, but it happened just as predicted. Robbie came awake and immediately asked for a knife. He told them that he wanted to cut an Easter egg and then he slipped back into his trance again. The prayers continued.

A few minutes later, the voice returned. "I will have ffiRobbie's real nameffl awake and ask for a drink of water." Robbie's eyes fluttered open and he asked for a drink of water. He drank the water that was offered to him and he closed his eyes and fell back onto the bed.

The Easter Sunday session continued on for several more hours and Father Bowdern began to realize that the holy day had been a turning point in the case. The prayers had ended with curses and threats from Robbie -- or whatever was pretending to be the boy. The voice -- the devil's voice, as Father Bishop called it -- began to come more and more frequently and began to speak with more authority. Robbie seemed to be completely under the control of it. Eyewitness accounts say that Robbie's "features became so contorted that he seemed altogether a different person."

And there was something else in the hospital room as well. Witnesses told of feeling a deep chill in the room and Father Bowdern found it especially hard to get warm. He began wearing an overcoat on top of his surplice and cassock. The men who assisted with the exorcism also told of a horrible stench that filled the room, just as it had in the rectory on a few occasions. The smell was so bad at time that witnesses had to leave and go out into the hall in order to breathe. These reports were similar to the accounts that emerged in later years from staff members at the hospital. They claimed that cold chills and strange smells would continue to manifest in and around the room for as long as it existed - even long after Robbie and the exorcists had departed.

The situation continued to intensify on Monday, April 18. Robbie woke up around 8:00 a.m., kicked the nurse at his bedside and jumped out of bed. Another monk ran into the room to assist him and Robbie seized a bottle of holy water from the desk. He threatened to throw the bottle at them and then threw it upward so that it shattered on the ceiling. The Alexians managed to get Robbie back into bed and started cleaning up the glass on the floor.

They were still cleaning when Father Widman arrived to see Robbie and to bring him Holy Communion. As he came over the bed, the boy spit in the chaplain's face. Father Widman slowly wiped it away and he urged Robbie -- if the boy was still himself -- to make a Spiritual Communion. Robbie replied by spitting at him again. The mucus and blood spattered the priest's face but as he wiped it away, he was convinced that he heard the sound of Robbie's voice. It was very quiet and faint but he was sure that he heard two words: "I can't."

Father Widman started to urge the boy again but before he could do so, Robbie spoke on his own. He spoke again in his own voice. "I want to receive you in Holy Communion...." he choked out and then fell back onto the bed.

Father Widman was relieved that the boy had made Spiritual Communion but before he could say another word, he heard that same horrible voice again, rumbling from Robbie's throat. Father Bishop recorded what the chaplain told him and according to what he heard, the message stated: "One devil is out. ffiRobbie's real nameffl must make nine communions and then I will leave."

Whatever Father Widman heard, he stayed in the room for another hour, trying to get Robbie to make nine more Spiritual Communions. Robbie seemed to be unable to speak, though, even after Father Widman shortened the words to "I wish to receive you..." Theologically speaking, this still should have been sufficient for a valid communion but Robbie could not get the words out. Instead, the voice of the devil, as Father Widman, believed it was, laughed at him.

"That isn't enough," the voice growled at him. "He has to say one more word, one little word.... He'll never say it. He has to make nine communions. He'll never say that word. I am always in him. I may not have much power always, but I am in him. He will never say that word."

Father Widman eventually gave up and left the room defeated and confused. What was the word? What could it be that could so easily free Robbie? And what was it that the demon would never allow him to say?

The day turned into a nightmare. Robbie began to sing obscene and horrible songs. He began urinating and threatening the Alexians, cursing at them and call them names. Then, abruptly, he calmed down and smiled. He asked for something to eat and then asked for a bath so that he could change out of his wet and stinking clothes. The brothers decided to wait for thirty minutes to see whether or not his mood changed again.

Just after noon, they brought him a tray with a piece of cake, some ice cream and a glass of milk. Robbie smiled and then snarled in rage. He grabbed the glass and hurled it against the wall. The tray was tossed aside and clattered onto the floor. The Alexians managed to get him back into his restraints and then none of them would go near him until later in the afternoon.

At that time, the Brothers brought another tray of food into the room and placed it on the desk across the room. They wanted to get Robbie out of bed so that they could bathe him, change the wet sheets and get him into a fresh pair of pajamas. Robbie seemed cooperative enough. He got up and walked to the desk, smiled and then picked up the plate that held a sandwich. He hurried quickly to the window and then turned to face the men in the room. Holding the plate in his hand as if he planned to launch it at any moment, he promised to hit anyone who dared to move.

One of the monks threw himself under the bed. Robbie laughed but the Brother had not been trying to escape. He slithered toward Robbie's feet and, when he started to seize them, another monk jumped forward and grabbed his arm. Robbie turned and threw the plate, which smashed against the wall. Several of the Alexians held onto him until his clothing and sheets could be changed.

Father Bowdern spent most of the day in meditation, re-reading the instructions in the *Rituale Romanum*. The exorcism seemed to be at an impasse. If anything, Robbie seemed to be getting worse. The devil continued to tease them with numbers and dates --- I will depart in ten days, it had told them, there are nine more devils in Robbie. The "X" that had appeared on his body, the numbers "4", "18", and more. Father Bowdern had placed so much hope on the liturgical calendar of Easter but that had been based on human reason and logic. Was that really what they were dealing with here?

Father Bowdern again plunged into the literature regarding possession, just as he did back when he first heard about Robbie's case. He learned of an 1870

142

case that took place in Wisconsin that seemed similar to Robbie's plight and he devised a new strategy. That evening, the ritual would resume and they would force Robbie to wear a chain of religious medals and to hold a crucifix in his hands. He was also determined to ask for the demon's responses in English, not Latin, which was the language of the possessed boy. If Robbie again claimed to be free of the devils, Father Bowdern would pay no attention to the claim. He would follow the instructions to the letter: "Yet the exorcist may not desist until he sees the signs of deliverance." The Jesuits would wait for a sign -- an unmistakable sign.

Father Bowdern telephoned Father Bishop and Father O'Flaherty and told them that they would be returning to the hospital at 7:00 p.m. With his new plan in mind, Father Bowdern was convinced that they would succeed.

When the priests entered the hospital room, they found Robbie being pinned to the bed by several Alexians. They had just carried him into the room, they explained. Just a short time before, Robbie had been seemingly normal and had asked if he could telephone his mother. They escorted him to a telephone but before they could reach it, he had turned wild again. He flailed and kicked and tried to claw at the eyes and throats of the monks. The men had managed to shove him to the floor and haul him back to his room, but Robbie had nearly escaped. At that point, no one had any idea what the boy would have done if he had been loose on the ward.

Father Bowdern began to read from the prayer book but instead of using his loud, commanding tone, he chose to read quietly instead. When the time came, he asked the demons, in Latin, for a sign that would tell of the day and hour of their departure. A moment later, he switched to English and said that the response should be given in that language.

Nothing happened. Robbie's head lolled to the side and he let out a growling moan, but nothing else.

Father Bowdern resumed the prayers in Latin and at one point, Robbie stirred and asked the meaning of some of the prayers. Father Bowdern explained and Robbie nodded and repeated the Latin words. Cheered slightly by Robbie's calmness and attention, Father Bowdern placed a crucifix in the boy's hands. Robbie screamed and began to thrash about on the bed. Two monks held him down but Robbie managed to get his hand freed and hurl the crucifix across the room.

The spell lasted for several minutes and then he seemed to come out of it again. He asked again about the Latin prayers and Father O'Flaherty suggested that he try to learn the Hail Mary in Latin. The priest began the words and within fifteen minutes or so, he was able to recite the prayer without help. Seizing the moment, the priest kept Robbie's attention by telling him the story of the children

143

who witnessed Our Lady of Fatima. Robbie paid close attention but that soon wavered. He asked for a Catholic reader for eighth graders and he thumbed through it, stopping occasionally to read part of a story. A moment later, he snapped the covers closed and balanced the book on his knees and then on his head.

Father O'Flaherty and Father Bowdern both realized that something seemed to be working. Robbie was suddenly more like himself - but not for long. The book was suddenly thrown across the room and Robbie's body slammed backwards onto the bed. His eyes were closed again and his body strained and contorted on the thin mattress.

This went on for some time and then suddenly, Robbie changed again. He said that he wanted to recite the rosary while the priests responded. Father Bowdern handed him the rosary and he clutched at it and began to pray in slow, faltering spurts. He recited the Apostle's Creed, the Our Father prayer, three Hail Mary's and more. He told the Jesuits that he felt the need to pray whenever he was able, asking if he could make Spiritual Communion on his own. He tried to do it and then Robbie was gone again.

His eyes squeezed shut and he thrashed about and cried that the religious medals that had been placed around his neck were hot. They were burning him, he whined, could he please take them off? Father Bowdern refused. Instead, he slipped a crucifix back into Robbie's hand again. This time, he did not throw it down.

Father Widman stepped to the bed, holding his most precious belonging, which was a crucifix that he had been given to him on the day he was ordained as a priest. He blessed Robbie and asked him to kiss the image of Jesus that was on the crucifix. Robbie barked at him exploded in a rage. He twisted his head away and tossed it back and forth as he howled and cursed the chaplain.

Then, he turned toward Father Bowdern and, according to a report from Father O'Flaherty, "spit into the exorcist's face with uncanny accuracy, invariably hitting the priest in the eyes." One of the Jesuits held a pillow between Robbie and Father Bowdern as a shield. Then, the report continued, "The boy's tongue began to flick out and his head to move to and fro in the gliding fashion of a snake. Suddenly, he would make a quick movement above, beneath, or alongside the pillow and spit mucus into the exorcist's eyes."

Father Bowdern recited the prayers incessantly for more than two hours as Robbie screamed and arched his body up off the bed. It took five of the Alexians to hold him down as he howled in what seemed to be pain and torment. At last, Father Bowdern read through the entire ritual one last time and then uttered the final "amen." Absolute silence filled the room. Robbie lay still on the bed and the exorcists hardly dared to breathe. Father Bishop checked his watch and later recorded the time. It was 10:45 p.m.

Robbie sucked in a long breath and then a new voice came from his lips. It was a loud, clear, masculine voice and one that was much different from the chilling voice the Jesuits had gotten so used to hearing. The voice claimed to be that of "St. Michael the Archangel" and it ordered the demon to depart. The voice shouted: "I command you Satan, and the other evil spirits to leave the body in the name of *Dominus*. Immediately! Now, now now!"

Father Bowdern suddenly realized what the word was that Robbie "would never say." It was *Dominus* -- that was the word.

Father Bishop's diary then went on to record "the most violent contortions of the entire period of exorcism." He called it a "fight to the finish" as Robbie's body went into a torrent of painful twists and spasms. Then, he fell quiet. A moment later, he sat up, smiled and then spoke in a normal voice. "He's gone", Robbie said, looking around at the priests and monks with the first real smile that any of them had seen from the boy in a long time.

The exorcism was finally over.

The Alexians rose from their prayerful postures and embraced one another. Father Bishop and Father O'Flaherty gripped one another by the shoulder and placed warm hands on Father Bowdern. Both men were smiling and they each waited for Father Bowdern's tears, his own smile and his prayers of thanks. But the exorcist was not smiling or crying --instead, he looked grim and tense. He was waiting for his sign. He had sworn not to give up until he received the sign that he had asked for.

As Father Bowdern brooded, Robbie seemed to come alive. He spoke with wonder of the "dream" that he had experienced. He told everyone that he had seen a wondrous figure, with long, flowing hair, that appeared from a bright while light. The figure wore a white robe that was covered with shining chain mail, as a knight would have worn in the Middle Ages. The figure, who Robbie believed was an angel, held a heavy sword that seemed to give off a bright glow. The man looked fierce and with the sword in one hand, he pointed with the other to a dark cave that was located a short distance away. From inside of the cavern, Robbie could see flames and fire and he could feel the heat from it. Just outside of the cave's entrance, was a demonic figure with misshapen features and a grotesque form. There were other creatures that lurked nearby.

The demon laughed at the angel as the shining figure ordered it to enter the cave. As it howled, the demon charged at the angel. Rather than raise his sword in defense, though, the angel merely turned and looked at Robbie with a smile on his face. He then turned back to the demon and spoke one word: "*Dominus*." The snarling creature screamed in agony, Robbie told of his dream, and then he and

145

the other demons vanished into the depths of the burning cave. The creatures descended into the darkness and then a metal gate slammed shut behind them with a loud clang. Robbie saw that letters had been welded into the gate. They spelled out the word "spite".

Robbie said that as the demons vanished, he felt a sharp tugging in his stomach and then something seemed to snap. When he awoke, he said that he felt that a huge pressure had been lifted off of him. The dark thoughts and depression that had overwhelmed him since January was suddenly gone. He couldn't remember the last time that he had felt so happy.

Robbie fell asleep a short time later and when he awoke the next morning, he repeated his dream to the Alexian who had stayed by his bed the night before. The monk helped him to dress and get cleaned up and Robbie prepared to attend Mass and to receive Holy Communion in the hospital chapel.

Father Van Roo said mass at the hospital that morning and when the time came for communion, Robbie joined the other patients and Alexians as they walked to the altar rail. He knelt there, raised his head and opened his mouth to receive the host. Father Van Roo felt a surge of joy as he placed the wafer on Robbie's tongue and the smiling boy received it in utter, almost serene, peace.

Robbie returned to his room after mass and although he had awakened late, laid down to take a nap in the afternoon. When he awoke, he seemed unable to remember anything about the ordeal that he had experienced over the past few months. In fact, when he first awoke, he had absolutely no idea where he was at all. He didn't recognize anyone at first, including Father Widman or the monks who had befriended him. That would change a short time later but for the most part, he remembered nothing of the possession or the horrible events that had occurred.

That memory lapse has continued to this day.

Moments after Robbie awakened, a booming sound was heard throughout the hospital. The large and thundering noise, like a small cannon being fired, was so intense that it could be heard in every part of the building. It was thought that perhaps something had exploded but nothing could be found that was damaged. One of the staff members later described it as a sound like that of an electrical transformer that had blown up. A search of the building revealed that nothing had occurred. What was the sound? No one knew, but it had apparently come from the fifth floor.

Brother Rector Cornelius, the head of the hospital, as well as a number of monks and staff members hurried to Robbie's room, fearing the worst. When they arrived, though, they found only Robbie, standing by the bed in the sunshine, a placid smile on his face. He had no idea what all of the fuss was about.

Father Bowdern finally had his sign.

PART FOUR:

AFTER THE EXORCISM

His Eminence has instructed me to inform you that he does not wish the case of the boy in Mount Rainier discussed publicly. The parents of the boy made a very strong request to that effect and we have tried to shield them and the boy from any embarrassing publicity.
1952 Letter from the Washington Archdiocese to a priest who requested information about the "Robbie Doe" case

Robbie left St. Louis with his parents twelve days after the exorcism ended and returned to Maryland. He wrote to Father Bowdern in May 1949 and told him that he was happy and had a new dog. Robbie was a normal, typical American boy of the late 1940s. No matter whether you believe in demons or possession or not, most can agree that "something" very strange happened to him in 1949. If you believe that he faked the whole thing, then consider the trauma that he must have experienced when the joke went too far and he found himself subjected to an exorcism, which was certainly not a pleasant experience. If you believe that he was truly possessed, or even mentally ill, then we have to consider him a victim of an unexplainable horror. The only person who knew what really happened during that terrible winter and spring was Robbie himself and he never spoke

147

about it again. Those who gently tried to prod his memory soon learned that he had only dim recollections of what had occurred anyway.

Robbie went on to attend a Catholic High School and remains a devout Catholic today. His parents also converted to Catholicism and received their first communion at Christmas of 1950. The boy of 1949 later went on to get married and to raise three children. There are a number of rumors that have swirled about him over the years, from the fact that he committed suicide to the claim that he was an American Airlines pilot. When I first began researching this story, the internet was in its infancy and the websites that have since revealed Robbie's real name did not exist. Through quite a bit of research in the late 1990s, I was able to learn the real identity of "Robbie Doe." Through a resource, I was able to make contact with him and at that time, I promised to never reveal who he was, or where he lived. His name is available now, but it never came from me. In fact, I find it shameful that people have chosen to put it into print. All that I will say about Robbie is that nothing supernatural ever occurred in his life again. He lived a normal life with an ordinary family and still lives in the Washington, D.C. area today.

Like Robbie, the Jesuits involved in the case went on to lead productive and mostly happy lives. None of the terrible death threats or predictions made by Robbie during the alleged possession ever came to pass. None of them were "burning in hell" in 1957 either. That dire warnings turned out to be just one of the many deceptions carried out by either the boy, or the demon, depending on what you believe.

Father Bowdern was convinced until the end of his life that he and his fellow priests had been battling a demonic entity. His supporters maintain that there were many witnesses to the alleged supernatural events that took place and that no other explanation existed for what was seen. A full report that was filed by the archdiocese stated that the case of Robbie Doe was a "genuine demonic possession." According to Father John Nicola, who had the opportunity to review the report, he noted that forty-eight persons had signed a document attesting to the fact that they had witnessed paranormal phenomena in the case.

The only church mention that was ever made of the exorcism was in the August 19, 1949 issue of the *Catholic Review*, a semi-official church publication. Archbishop Joseph E. Ritter of St. Louis appointed a Jesuit professor to conduct an investigation, but the results were never made public. Ritter asked his subordinates to stop talking about the incident after receiving the report because, according to the source, "It's not that they were hiding anything. It just was that they felt that the overall effect of the thing was counterproductive."

As mentioned, Father Bowdern never publicly spoke of the exorcism, both to protect Robbie's privacy and also because he didn't feel that it was right to do so.

As he told Father Walter Halloran: "Make a statement about it and you'd have a whole group of people who would want to destroy it, and you'd have another group of people who would want to make it a true exorcism. I don't think they ffiChurch authoritiesffl are ever going to say a word about it. I think they will never say whether it was or it wasn't. You and I know it. We were there."

Father Bowdern took the knowledge of the exorcism with him to the grave. He remained the pastor of St. Francis Xavier until 1956, went on to other assignments, ending his career back at the same church as confessor. And while he never spoke of what happened in 1949, there are rumors that he may have performed another exorcism before he retired. In June 1950, the bishop of Stuebenville, Ohio, aware of the 1949 St. Louis Exorcism, wrote to Archbishop Ritter and asked for help. The Ohio bishop said that a young man in the Stuebenville archdiocese was attacking priests and nuns and it was believed that he might be possessed. Ritter, through his chancellor, asked Bowdern to look into the matter but there is no further information as to what might have occurred after that. Father Bowdern passed away in 1983 at the age of 86.

Father Raymond Bishop, after twenty-two years at St, Louis University, was sent to Creighton University in Omaha, Nebraska. He taught here for more than twenty years and died in 1978 at the age of 72.

Father O'Flaherty served as the pastor and the assistant pastor of St. Francis Xavier and other churches until 1976, when he went into retirement at Regis College in Denver, Colorado. He died of pneumonia at St. Louis University Hospital in 1987 at the age of 80.

Walter Halloran was a seminary student at the time of the exorcism and he was present during the sessions held at the house on Roanoke Drive, at the St Francis Xavier rectory and at the Alexian Brothers Hospital. He was not there at the culmination of the events at the hospital but he had seen and witnessed enough to make him an excellent witness to what occurred. Because of this, he had appeared in dozens of articles that had been written about the case by the time that I began doing my own research into the story.

Following the events that have been chronicled here, Walter Halloran was ordained as a priest in 1954. Two years later, he began teaching history and theology and coaching football at the Campion Jesuit High boarding school in Prairie du Chien, Wisconsin. Between 1963 and 1966, he taught history at Marquette University and then in 1966, he volunteered for the U.S. Army and began serving as a chaplain. He initially served in Germany but at the age of 48, volunteered for paratrooper duty and then went on to Vietnam in 1969. He earned two Bronze Stars for his heroic efforts during the war.

In 1971, Father Halloran left the service and returned to St. Louis University as assistant director of campus ministry and then as alumni director. He went on to a variety of assignments in Minnesota and California and during this time became a reluctant celebrity when word leaked out that *The Exorcist* was based on a true story. Father Halloran never sought fame and frankly, didn't want it. But he did speak out many times about what happened in St. Louis in 1949.

I found that Father Halloran had made some conflicting at best statements about the exorcism over the years. On one hand, he had stated that he was not convinced that Robbie exhibited any sort of unnatural strength when he was "possessed." He said that he was punched by the boy several times and believed it to be nothing more than the strength that an agitated adolescent could summon. Perhaps in contemplation, Father Halloran later reversed some of his comments and told an interviewer that while he was not an expert enough in the field to make a determination as to whether the possession was officially genuine or not, he did believe that it was real. "I have always thought in my mind that it was," he said.

In addition, while being interviewed on the show of popular St. Louis radio Dave Glover, Halloran dismissed the idea that, as in the movie, Robbie ever levitated off the bed. However, he did add that on several occasions, the iron bed that the boy was on did actually levitate off the floor. He also described the "skin writings" that had appeared on Robbie's legs and chest and expressed that he had no natural explanation for them.

In early 2005, I was able to contact Father Halloran and found him to be a warm, genuine and friendly man. Although I expected him to be quite tired of talking about the story of Robbie Doe, he gladly related the story to me when I explained that I was looking for as much truth in the story as I could find. Much of what has been included in this book came from four different interviews that Father Halloran was kind enough to grant me.

Of course, I asked him the inevitable question as to whether or not he believed the possession was authentic and he paused for a moment before he answered. "I can't say whether or not it was valid. At one time, I felt more strongly in one way than another but I simply don't know. I have never been convinced that it fit all of the criteria of a true possession but there was something going on there that I could not explain. For this reason, and others, I have withheld judgment on the matter. Father Bowdern always believed in the case but I have never been comfortable with any decision."

I asked Father Halloran whether or not he believed Robbie could have faked his symptoms. He answer to this was without doubt. "No," he replied. "I have never felt that he faked any of it. He was a nice kid. What happened, I can't say, but it was not a hoax."

"Do you think that it could have been caused by a mental illness?" I asked him.

"Perhaps," Father Halloran replied. "I have always thought that, taken one at a time, many of the incidents could be explained as being psychosomatic but the dilemma comes when you put them all together. I don't know if a mental illness can explain all of that."

My last interview with Father Halloran took place in January 2005 and I learned a short time later, on March 1, that he had passed away from cancer at the age of 83. He had been living at the St. Camillus Jesuit community in Wauwatosa, Wisconsin at the time of his death.

The last living link to the 1949 St. Louis Exorcism case was gone.

We know what happened to most of those who were involved in the case, but what about the case itself? What really happened and most importantly, what possessed Robbie Doe? There are a number of theories that have been floating around for decades and we'll take a look at each of these:

THE HOAX

Many believe that Robbie may have been faking the whole thing. Mark Opsasnick, during his research into the boy's troubled childhood, began to feel that the case may have started as a way to get attention, or to get out of school, and that it snowballed into the mess that it became. While he does some great investigative work into the early stages of the case, and does have many relevant points about Robbie's childhood and the many flaws in the chronicling of the case, he is too quick to dismiss some of the strange things that occurred in front of multiple witnesses. His report never delves at all into the events in St. Louis and in this way, leaves out just about everything that took place that was so hard to explain.

Based on what he uncovered about some of the erroneous "facts" in the case, namely the "attack" on Father Hughes, Opsasnick was certainly justified in having doubts about the validity of the entire thing. However, he is quick to dismiss some of Robbie's spells as "seizures" and as mentioned, he never investigated anything that occurred in St. Louis. He also dismissed the entire "exorcist's diary" as being merely what Father Bishop imagined the entire case to be. Opsasnick did great work on this case but never approached it with the open mind that was needed -- nor as completely as he should have -- when he decided that the case could not be authentic. His fatal mistake was to state that he "did not believe in the case" and I say that only because he was not there to witness it for himself. I can't say whether I believe in it or not. All that I can do is present the story as it has been told and allow the reader to judge for himself.

I feel that perhaps I am being unfair to Mark Opsasnick in singling him out as a "non-believer" in the authenticity of the case. There are many who are unwilling to believe in the possibility of the case and not surprisingly, skepticism runs rampant when it comes to these events. It should be noted, though, that people who have suggested that all of this was nothing more than a hoax, are all people who were in no way involved in the case. The opinions of the priests who were present, the workers and monks at Alexian Brothers and others who were there during most of the events that took place have to be considered and acknowledged far beyond those who speculate and yet were not even born in 1949.

POLTERGEIST?

Some would agree that while Robbie was not possessed, he was afflicted with another unexplainable paranormal disturbance. Earlier in the book, I mentioned "poltergeist" activity in connections with possession, but that's not the only time it occurs. On its own, it is a genuine paranormal phenomenon.

The current theory behind this activity that it's caused by a person in the household, known as the "human agent." The agent is usually an adolescent and normally one that is troubled emotionally. It is believed that they can unconsciously manipulate physical objects in the house by psychokinesis PK , the power to move things by energy generated in the brain. This kinetic type of energy remains unexplained, but some mainstream scientists have started to explore the idea that it might exist.

It is unknown why this energy seems to appear in young people around the age of puberty, but documentation of its existence have started to become public. It seems that when the activity begins to manifest, the agent is usually in the midst of some emotional or sexual turmoil. The presence of the energy is almost always an unconscious one and it is rare when any of the agents actually realize that they are the source of the destruction around them. They do not realize that they are the reason that objects in the home have become displaced and are usually of the impression that a ghost or some sort of other supernatural entity is present instead. The bursts of PK come and go and most poltergeist-like cases will peak early and then slowly fade away.

It should be noted that while most cases such as this manifest around young women, it is possible for puberty age boys and even older adults to show this same unknowing ability.

While medical doctors have little interest in this phenomenon, a few more adventurous scientists have grudgingly speculated that perhaps the human mind has abilities and energies that are still unrecognized. These energies just might be able to make objects move, writing to appear on skin and beds to shake. If it can really happen, it just might explain what happen to Robbie Doe. After the case had ended, this turned out to be Rev. Luther Schulze's theory about what happened in Maryland.

Some have theorized that Robbie's unhappy childhood created a situation of repression and anger that may have caused poltergeist phenomena to occur. It is thought that when the activity began, his superstitious family first came to believe that their house was haunted by "Aunt Tillie" and then came to believe that Robbie was possessed by demons. Poltergeist phenomena could have caused such things as mysterious knockings and scratching, the shaking bed, objects that moved about and more. Perhaps as the "possession scenario" was intensified, Robbie grew more and more upset, causing more and more activity to take place.

As mentioned, Reverend Schulze did not believe that Robbie was possessed. Based on what he witnessed in his home, Robbie was manifesting paranormal energy that caused physical objects to be displaced. He even went as far as to contact scientist J.B. Rhine, who pioneered research into PK energy. Rhine agreed that what he heard sounded like a "classic poltergeist case." Rhine later traveled to Washington to observe the phenomena taking place but by this time, Robbie and his family had left for St. Louis.

Could this case have been nothing more than a "poltergeist gone berserk"?

It certainly seems plausible on the surface, just as the hoax theory does -- but only to a point and only if we ignore the "exorcist's diary" and everything that happened in St. Louis. If any of what was reported by the later witnesses, and the Jesuits, can be taken seriously, then poltergeist activity cannot begin to explain what happened to Robbie.

MENTAL ILLNESS OR POSSESSION?

Many feel that Robbie suffered from a mental illness and not demonic possession. He may have been hallucinating or suffering from some weird psychosomatic illness that caused him to behave so strangely, to curse and scream and to thrash about so violently. Did the religious belief of the Jesuits hide the fact that Robbie was dangerously ill?

To this day, the Church has never stated one way or another as to whether or not Robbie was possessed by demons, despite what seems to be enough evidence to make, or break, the case. The "diary", chronicled by a priest, is the most detailed account of possession in modern times and there are also believed to be reports in the files of two archdioceses and in the files of the Jesuits as well. Father John Nicola, who claimed to read one of these documents, stated that it was signed by forty-eight witnesses, including nine Jesuits, who saw Robbie in the throes of possession. The Church has enough information to make a judgment on the case and yet the small story in The *Catholic Review* is the only Catholic-related report that has ever been made.

In the report, though, all of the witnesses who signed the statement confirming that they believed in the authenticity of the case, an examiner appointed by Archbishop Ritter did not. The examiner, who interviewed participants in the matter, concluded that Robbie was not the victim of demonic possession. He added in reports from two psychiatrists from Washington University who said they saw no evidence of the supernatural. The examiner went with the "poltergeist" theory and after that, Archbishop Ritter stopped everyone from talking about the case, believing that it was "counterproductive." The examiner's report was never released.

Father Halloran later recalled that his friend, Father Bowdern, spoke about the matter to him and said that he did not believe an official statement would ever be made. If a statement would be made, it would divide the Church into those who believed that it was not a true possession and those who believed it was. Father Bowdern believed that it was genuine, however. He was there, he said, and he had seen it.

But what had Father Bowdern and the others really seen? Was it a demon? Was it evil?

The idea of "evil" has been with us since the dawn of man and in Christian culture it has long been connected to the powerful fallen angels, led by Satan, who had the ability to torment -- and possess -- human beings. In the New Testament, it was learned that demons could be expelled by Jesus and later by his followers. They were driven out by God's will through the name of Jesus.

At the time of Christ, there was a belief that demons caused mental illness. The power to cast out these demons was a great power -- it was a power to heal. The ancient concept of possession was much like the modern conception of mental illness. There was little difference between them, which has led many to believe that even the exorcisms conducted by Jesus were the result of a misunderstanding. It has been ventured that an error may have occurred because the words "devil" and "demons" were thought to be interchangeable. Some interpretations of the Bible say that "possessed by demons" should actually read "afflicted by harmful forces" or even by "evil spirits." A modern version of that phrase would be that "I'm in bad spirits today."

With this in mind, it is thought that perhaps the exorcisms of Jesus were actually cures of diseases and not true exorcisms. When the possessed were healed, the invisible cause, which was translated incorrectly as a "devil" was expelled and so the long tradition of exorcisms by casting out demons by Jesus had begun. Those who favor this explanation for possession believe that Robbie's case was another example of a mentally ill person who was erroneously thought to be possessed, just like so many people were in ancient times.

But the belief in possession is not confined to centuries past. There are many people from various cultures, in modern times, who believe they can be taken over by evil spirits. No matter what culture these people may have come from, they also have a ritual that can exorcize these creatures.

In modern America, where psychiatry is a healing force, psychiatrists become "exorcists" of sorts. As mentioned earlier in this book, many experts point to a multiple personality disorder as a cause for so-called "demonic possession." Many such patients come to believe in some sort of being inside of them, causing them to do and say things that they might not otherwise. Could Robbie have been afflicted with this sort of disorder? It seems unlikely but it could be possible, despite the fact that true cases of Multiple Personality Disorder are nearly as rare as those who are truly possessed.

Some experts have suggested Tourette's syndrome as an explanation for Robbie's "possession." Those who have this illness uncontrollably curse and scream, grunt and twitch and may involuntarily shout out curses, filthy language and even death threats. This seems like a possibility until we consider the fact that whatever was wrong with Robbie, it was cured. At this time, there is no cure for Tourette's syndrome and there was certainly no cure in 1949.

There are also those who believe that Robbie's "possession" was the result of a rare mental illness known as childhood schizophrenia. In most cases, schizophrenia is a disorder that manifests later in the teenage years or in early adulthood. But there have been cases of boys who develop normally until about the age of ten and then suddenly start hearing voices and reacting violently. Again, this at first seems to be a possibility until we consider the fact that Robbie was somehow "cured" of his illness without any sort of medical treatment or medication.

So, what really happened to Robbie? We'll never know for sure but despite the skeptics that exist, offering their mundane explanations for what occurred, there were and are many who believe the events were real. They have no explanation for what took place in 1949 and cannot deny the memories of those events that still linger today.

PART FIVE:

...AND INTO HISTORY

HOW THE 1949 CASE BECAME "THE EXORCIST"

In 1949, while a Junior at Georgetown University in Washington D.C., I read in the August 20 edition of the Washington Post the following account..... The article impressed me. And coolly understated that is. I wasn't just impressed; I was excited. For hear at least, in this city, in my time, was tangible evidence of transcendence. If there were demons, there were angels and probably a God and a life everlasting. And thus it occurred to me long afterward, when I'd started my career as a writer, that this case of possession which had joyfully haunted my hopes in the years since 1949 was the worthwhile subject of a novel.
William Peter Blatty

While the Jesuit community, out of respect for Bowdern and Archbishop Ritter, kept the secret of the exorcism, Reverend Luther Schulze in Maryland had no responsibility to do so. Soon after the family returned home in April, Schulze noticed that they were not coming to his church on Sundays. He stopped by to see them and learned that Robbie had converted to Catholicism that his parents planned to follow suit. Schulze apparently felt that the conversion released him from any confidential relationship that he had with them and so on August 9, he told a meeting of the Washington, D.C. branch of the Society for Parapsychology that he had witnessed a "poltergeist" in the home of a "Mr. and Mrs. John Doe," who lived in a Washington suburb. He used Robbie's actual first name and told them of the strange manifestations that he had seen in his home. He added that the boy was later taken to a city in the Midwest but did not speak of the exorcism, which he had no real information about.

But somehow, the secret leaked out anyway. News of a poltergeist outbreak reached the newspapers and Schulze made himself available for interviews. No exorcism was ever mentioned in the article, which kept the identities secret, but somehow, one of the accounts garbled the remarks from the meeting that Schulze attended and reported that three exorcisms had taken place in the Midwestern city. The idea of an exorcism was so much more interesting to the newspapers that the poltergeist story was abandoned in favor of the alleged exorcisms. Reporters began calling contacts at the archdiocese in Washington and the queries started a chain of events. A spokesman for Archbishop O'Boyle in Washington refused to provide any information to the press but, as mentioned, details ended up being leaked to the *Catholic Review*, the nationally syndicated paper. In the edition that was dated on August 19, a three-paragraph story appeared under a Washington dateline. It read:

A 14 year-old Washington boy whose history of diabolical possession was widely reported in the press last week, was successfully exorcised by a priest after being received into the Catholic Church, it was learned here.

The priest refused to discuss the case in any way. However, it is known that several attempts had been made to free the boy of the manifestations.

A Catholic priest was called upon for help. When the boy expressed the desire to enter the church, with the consent of his parents he received religious instruction. Later the priest baptized him and then successfully performed the ritual of exorcism. The parents of the afflicted boy are non-Catholics.

Strangely, at that point, though, the possession had not been "widely reported" and the brief article seemed to be little more than an attempt by the Church to control the story. As it turned out though, it only whetted the appetites of the Washington press. Jeremiah O'Leary, an assistant city editor for the *Washington Star-News*, spotted the story and began trying to track down information. He later admitted that he called every priest that he knew before finally publishing a short story that was printed on the afternoon of August 19 on an inside page of the paper. The following day, the *Washington Post* printed a long and detailed story about the exorcism on the front page reprinted here

157

in the introduction to this book . They reported that the exorcism occurred in both Washington and St. Louis and had been carried out by "a Jesuit in his 50's". The secret of the exorcism was finally out.

"Exorcist" author William Peter Blatty

One of the readers of the newspaper stories was William Peter Blatty, an undergraduate at Georgetown University. Blatty, who was then in his junior year, was considering becoming a Jesuit. He became a writer instead and in 1970, began work on a book that would be based on the stories that he heard about the exorcist's "diary" and the articles that he read in college.

Father Bishop's "diary" of the Robbie Doe case came to light in the fall of 1949 under rather odd circumstances. Father Eugene B. Gallagher, S.J., who was on the faculty of Georgetown, was lecturing on the topic of exorcisms when one of his students, the son of a psychiatrist at St. Elizabeth's Hospital in Washington, spoke of a diary that had been kept by the Jesuits involved in the Robbie Doe exorcism. Father Gallagher asked the psychiatrist, who may have been one of the professionals involved in the early stages of the case, for a copy of the diary and eventually received a sixteen-page document that was titled "Case Study by Jesuit Priests." It had apparently been intended to be used a guide for future exorcisms.

While he was in college, Blatty asked to see a copy of the "diary," but his request was refused. Years later, he turned back to newspapers for information about the case and managed to track down the name of the priest involved. His name was Rev. William S. Bowdern, S.J. of St. Louis. Father Bowdern refused to comment on the case for the newspaper reports, as priests who perform exorcisms are said to be sworn to secrecy. Blatty tried contacting him anyway but the priest refused to cooperate. Out of respect, Blatty changed the identity of the possession victim in his book to a young girl, but the exorcist of the novel remains an apparently thinly veiled portrait of Father Bowdern.

Father Bowdern passed away in 1983, never publicly acknowledging the fact that he was involved in the St. Louis case. He had talked with other Jesuits, though, and eventually these stories reached a man named Thomas Allen, an author and contributing editor to *National Geographic*. He managed to find one of the participants in the case, Father Walter Halloran, S.J., who was then living in a small town in Minnesota. Father Halloran was suspicious at first but he did admit that there had been a "diary." But was it the "diary" that fell into the hands of Father Gallagher? Maybe or maybe not...

According to legend, the diary that Father Halloran had access to later turned up as a twenty-six-page document of the case that was literally snatched out of the old Alexian Brothers hospital just before it was demolished. So, where did the sixteen-page diary come from? And what happened to it? Accounts have it that Father Gallagher later loaned his sixteen-page diary to Father Brian McGrath, S.J., then dean of Georgetown University, in the spring of 1950. When Gallagher later tried to retrieve the diary, he was told that seven pages of the diary had been lost. Only nine of the sixteen pages remained and they were only photocopies.

And what about the later twenty-six-page diary? Sources say that this longer document was found in the Alexian Brothers Hospital on South Broadway in St. Louis. The old psychiatric wing of the hospital was being torn down in 1978 and workmen were sent in to remove furniture from that part of the building. One of these men found the document in a desk drawer of a locked room and he gave it to his supervisors, who in turn passed it on to hospital administrators. It was eventually identified as the work of Rev. Raymond Bishop, S.J., a priest who had participated in the exorcism. The manuscript was locked away but Father Halloran had access to it. He made a copy of the diary and sent it to Allen, who published a book about it in 1993.

Author William Peter Blatty never had access to the actual "diary" but as mentioned earlier, he did manage to track down Father Bowdern as he was doing research for his book but the Jesuit did not want to talk about the case. He did mention to him that yes, there had been a "diary" but he could not help him because of his promise of secrecy and the fear that any further publicity might disturb Robbie's life, even after more than two decades.

"My own thoughts," Bowdern later wrote to Blatty, "were that much good might have come if the case had been reported, and people had come to realize that the presence and the activity of the devil is something very real. And possibly never more real than at the present time... I can assure you of one thing: The case in which I was involved was the real thing. I had no doubt about it then and I have no doubt about it now."

At Bowdern's request, Blatty fictionalized the events of the exorcism and actually used the more lurid elements of the 1928 Iowa Exorcism to round out his book. To further hide the identity of Robbie, he changed the possessed victim to a young girl and moved the entire sequence from St. Louis to Washington. The exorcist in the book, however, Father Merrin, was definitely based on William Bowdern.

In 1971, Blatty's book *The Exorcist* appeared in print and became an instant bestseller. There was immediate talk of a film version and Blatty was hired to do the script. The book was loved by critics and readers alike but the author struggled with the script, tossing away a number of re-writes of his original text before finally coming with a version that satisfied the director of the project, William Friedkin. Blatty had wanted Friedkin as the director because he was well-known for his documentary work and Blatty felt strongly that the story needed "somebody who could give the film a sense of reality." The resulting film was a solid financial success and is remembered today as one of the most terrifying films ever made.

The filming of *The Exorcist* was done over a nine-month period. The main set, a reproduction of the Georgetown home, was built in a warehouse in New York. During the filming, a number of curious incidents and accidents took place involving the set and those involved with the production. In addition, the budget of the film rose from $5 million to more than twice that amount. Obviously, any film production that lasts for more than a month or so will have mishaps and accidents occur but the production of *The Exorcist* seems to have been particularly affected but some unforeseeable calamities. The first occurred around 2:30 a.m. one Sunday morning when a fire broke out on the set. There was only one security guard at the Ceco 54th Street Studios when the McNeil house set caught fire and burned. The fire was the result of a bad electric circuit but it shut down filming for six weeks while the set was constructed again from scratch. Ironically, as soon as the new set was ready, the sprinkler system broke down, causing an additional two-week delay.

Few of the actors in the film escaped personal troubles during the shoot. Just as Max Von Sydow Father Merrin touched down in New York to film his first scenes, his brother died unexpectedly in Sweden. Von Sydow himself later became very ill during the filming. Irish actor Jack MacGowran Burke Dennings died only one week after his character was killed by the demon in the movie. Jason Miller Father Karras was stunned when his young son Jordan was struck down on an empty beach by a motorcyclist who appeared out of nowhere. The boy almost died. Ellen Burstyn Chris McNeill wrenched her back badly during one scene when she was slapped by the possessed girl. The stunt went badly awry and she was laid up in bed for several weeks afterward, causing more delays in the filming.

In New York, one of the carpenters accidentally cut off his thumb on the set and one of the lighting technicians lost a toe. The location trip to Iraq was delayed from the spring, which is relatively cool, to July, the hottest part of the summer, when the temperature rose to 130 degrees and higher. Out of the eighteen man crew that was sent there, Friedkin lost the services of nine of them, at one time or another, due to dysentery or sunstroke. To make matters worse, the bronze statue of the neo-Assyrian winged demon Pazazu, which was packed in a ten-foot crate, got lost in an air shipment from Los Angeles and ended up in Hong Kong, which caused another two-week delay.

"I don't know if it was a jinx, really," actress Ellen Burstyn later said. "But there were some really strange goings-on during the making of the film. We were dealing with some really heavy material and you don't fool around with that kind of material without it manifesting in some way. There were many deaths on the film. Linda's grandfather died, the assistant cameraman's wife had a baby that died, the man who refrigerated the set died, the janitor who took care of the building was shot and killed ... I think overall there were nine deaths during the course of the film, which is an incredible amount... it was scary."

Things got so bad that William Friedkin took some drastic measures. Father Thomas Bermingham, S.J., from the Jesuit community at Fordham University, had been hired as a technical advisor for the film, along with Father John Nicola, who, while not a Jesuit, had been taught by Jesuit theologians at St. Mary of the Lake Seminary in Mundelein, Illinois. Friedkin came to Bermingham and asked him to exorcize the set. The priest was unable to perform an actual exorcism but he did give a solemn blessing in a ceremony that was attended by everyone then on the set, from Max Von Sydow to the technicians and grips. "Nothing else happened on the set after the blessing," Bermingham stated, "but around that time, there was a fire in the Jesuit residence set in Georgetown."

And while nothing else tragic occurred on the set, strange events and odd coincidences were reported during the post-production work on the film. "There were strange images and visions that showed up on film that were never planned," Friedkin later claimed. "There are double exposures in the little girl's face at the end of one reel that are unbelievable."

The film opened on December 26, 1973 to massive crowds. Within weeks of the first public screenings of the film, stories started to make the rounds that audience members were fainting and vomiting in the theaters. There were also reports of disturbing nightmares and reportedly, a number of theater ushers had to be placed under a doctor's care, or quit their jobs, after experiencing successive showings of the movie. In numerous cities that were checked after *The Exorcist* had run for several weeks, reporters found that every major hospital had been forced to deal with patients who reported, after seeing the film, severe cases of vomiting and hallucinations. There were also reports of people being carried out of theater in stretchers. Mere publicity tactics, or the real thing?

The film created a widespread interest in exorcism but the result of this was often questionable. Scores of already disturbed people began showing up at churches with claims of being possessed, while their problems should have been attributed to mental illness instead. In addition, renegade priests and self-proclaimed holy men started billing themselves as "exorcists" and "demonologists," hoping to cash in on the popularity of the film and the widespread interest in the occult that followed its release.

Rumors and half-truths have surrounded this film for years, including the most controversial one of all -- that actual demonic voices recorded during an exorcism were mixed into the soundtrack. Friedkin did admit that he was in the possession on a "cassette recording of an actual exorcism performed in Rome. It's in Italian. It involves the exorcism of a 14 year-old boy. I got the tape through the Jesuit Provincial of New York and on the tape are the sounds produced by this young man supposedly possessed." While Friedkin never claims to have used the sounds in the film, he does claim that he emulated them on the soundtrack for the demon. It has been this rumor that has provoked angry claims that *The Exorcist* is somehow dangerous or evil. Some fundamentalists have claimed that there is evil in the very celluloid of the film itself.

While such claims are unlikely, at best, there have been many people over the years who have felt that there are places -- and objects -- that continue to embody the very real evil that was expelled in 1949.

PART SIX:

THE DEVIL IN ST. LOUIS

We went down into the basement, just where the priest told us to go, and he took us back to a room of the cellar that was locked up --- there was a door lock and a big padlock too, I remember that. Inside of the room was all of this furniture that had been draped with cloth. He wanted us to load it all up and take it to a storage unit but I do remember one thing --- the priest refused to go into the room where the furniture was. In fact, he looked really scared to even stand in the doorway of it.
Interview Subject who claimed to move the furniture from the Alexian Hospital's "Exorcism Room"

When Robbie left the Alexian Brothers Hospital, Brother Rector Cornelius went to the fifth floor corridor of the old wing, turned a key in the door and stated that the room was to be kept permanently locked. From that day on, the Alexian Brothers in St. Louis maintained the secrets of the exorcism. The existence of Father Bishop's diary also remained a secret and a copy of it had been placed inside of the room when it was sealed. Everyone who worked in the hospital, though, knew why the room was locked. For years after the exorcism, people who were involved in the case, or who worked at the hospital, shared stories of things they heard and saw during the several week ordeal that occurred in the psychiatric wing. Orderlies spoke of cleaning up pools of vomit and urine in the boy's rooms. Staff members and nurses claimed to hear the sounds of someone screaming and the echoes of demonic laughter coming from Robbie's room. Most especially, though, they spoke of the cold waves of air that seemed to emanate from the room. No matter how warm the rest of the hospital was, the area around the door to the boy's room was always ice cold.

And even after the exorcism ended, something apparently remained behind. Was it some remnant of the entity that possessed Robbie or perhaps the impression of the horrific events that occurred in the room? Whatever it was, the room was never re-opened. Electrical problems plagued the surrounding rooms and it was always cold in the hallway outside the door to this particular room. The entire section of the hospital was eventually closed but whether or not this was because of the "exorcism room" is unknown.

As the years passed, tales about the locked room were passed on to new monks, nurses and orderlies who came to serve at the hospital. They knew that the room was located in a wing for extremely ill mental patients but did not understand why one room was kept sealed --- until they heard about what had happened there. The Alexians who had been on the staff in 1949 would not soon forget what they had seen and heard.

In the early 1950s, one of the monks was working at a boy's summer camp that was operated by the St. Louis archdiocese near Hillsboro, Missouri. He was a gentle, friendly man and was well-liked by the boys because of his demeanor and his massive size. One afternoon, the burly monk was sitting at a table in the mess hall with several of the young men and they were talking and laughing and paying little attention to a radio that was playing in the background.

Then, a song came on that used the theme of the Woody Woodpecker cartoons -- a song that that had Woody's jangling and rather maniacal laugh. The large Alexian lunged across the table and roughly yanked the radio's electrical cord out of the socket. Trembling and breaking out in a cold sweat, he simply told his companions that he couldn't stand the song. Later on, though, he told them about night after night in the spring of 1949 when he and the other monks were kept awake by wild, chilling laughter -- that sounded a lot like Woody Woodpecker -- coming from one of the rooms in the old wing of the Alexian Brothers Hospital.

Other Alexians had their own stories to tell. They spoke of banging sounds on their doors at night, voices calling in the darkened corridors, and more. Staff members would continue the stories in the years to come and I have personally spoken to more than a dozen nurses, maintenance people, orderlies and doctors who have dark and distinct memories of the old wing and the locked room on the psychiatric floor. Some of them have told me that sometimes -- even after all of these years -- they still dream about that wing and that one locked door.

The stories and tales about the "St. Louis Exorcism" have continued to circulate over the years and many of the stories have involved the physical locations that were connected to the case. One of them, the old rectory of the St. Francis Xavier Church, was torn down many years ago and in 1978, the old Alexian Brothers Hospital became a memory as well.

But the stories of this lost part of St. Louis has continued to haunt many hearts and minds as the years have passed.

In May 1976, work began on a new Alexian Brothers Hospital and in the first phase of the construction, some of the old outbuildings were torn down and a new six-story tower with two-story wings was built. In October 1978, the patients were moved out of the original hospital building and the contractor ordered the structure to be razed. It was done, but not without difficulty. Workers on the demolition crew claimed to be unable to control the wrecking ball when that floor was taken off. The ball swung around and hit a portion of a new building but luckily did no damage. This incident seemed to further enhance the legend of the room -- a legend which continued to grow.

Before the demolition was started, workers first combed through the building for old furniture that was to be taken out and sold. One of them found a locked room in the psychiatric wing and broke in. The room was fully furnished with a dust-covered bed, nightstand, chairs and a desk table with a single drawer. Before removing the table, the worker curiously opened the drawer to see what was inside. He found a small stack of papers inside.

The furniture, including all of the items in the locked room, was sold to a company that owned a nursing home a short distance away from the hospital. All of that which was salvaged from the hospital was locked in a room on the fourth floor of the nursing home and was never used. The nursing home itself was later torn down and many of these demolition workers, like the staff people and the city inspectors who had come through, refused to go on the fourth floor -- and were never able to explain why. What became of the furniture from the locked room is unknown.

Or at least that's one version of the story...

In recent years, another, stranger version about the fate of the items within the room has come to light. According to sources, the furniture was removed from the locked room at the time of the demolition but was never sold to the nursing home with the rest of it. The bed, nightstand, chairs and desk table were instead moved and locked away in the basement of a rectory in St. Louis. A number of years later, the rectory was scheduled to be torn down and movers were brought to haul away a number of items that were left in the basement. According to one of them, he arrived at the rectory with some other workers and they were taken down into the basement by a priest. He unlocked a door to one of the rooms in the back and let the men inside of it. However, the worker distinctly remembered that the priest himself refused to set foot inside. Within the room, they found several pieces of furniture that they were directed to remove and then seal up into a wooden crate. After that, the crate was to be placed in a storage facility and locked. The movers completed the task and then moved the crate to a storage warehouse that is located almost directly across from the gates to Scott Air Force base in Illinois. According to his story, the furniture from the "Exorcism Room," as it became known, is still here, sealed in a crate and largely forgotten.

As for the papers the workmen found inside of the room, though, they were far from forgotten. The manuscript appeared to be some sort of journal or diary and there was a letter attached to them that had been written to a Brother Cornelius that was dated for April 29, 1949. A portion of it read: "The enclosed report is a summary of the case which you have known for the past several weeks. The Brother's part of this case has been so very important that I thought you should have the case history for your permanent file". It was signed by Father Raymond J. Bishop, a Jesuit from St. Louis University. Apparently, Brother Cornelius considered the record best kept in secret, inside of the sealed room.

The worker took the papers to his boss, the contractor for the demolition, who then passed them on to the administrator of the hospital, a layman. The administrator read the letter in bewilderment but then started to turn the pages of the diary. As he began to scan through it, he began to see references to exorcism and realized that the diary spelled out all of the secrets of the locked room. His daughter, who was attending secretarial school and helping out in her father's office, managed to get a look at the paper before the administrator locked them away. She recognized the name "Walter Halloran" in the text because he was an uncle of one of her classmates. The administrator made contact with the former seminary student, now a Jesuit priest, and passed on the papers to him. The diary was then allegedly sealed in a safety deposit box but only after a carbon copy was made of it. It is this copy that has been circulated today and provides what little, and often confusing, information that we have on the 1949 exorcism.

St. Louis legend has it though that this was not the strangest thing to happen when the locked room was opened. According to crew members who worked for the Department of Transportation, "something" was seen emerging from the room just moments before the wrecking ball claimed it. Whatever it was, the men likened it to a "cat or a big rat or something." I wouldn't begin to suggest what this creature might have been, natural or supernatural, but I will say that it has continued to add to the legend of the "St. Louis Exorcism Case" over the years.

The old Alexian Brothers Hospital has vanished into history --- gone but not forgotten. However, there is another location in St. Louis that was just as closely connected to the exorcism but has been largely ignored over the years. It was a place where many of the most horrific events of the possession took place and where the Jesuits spent countless hours to rid Robbie Doe of whatever dark forces had inhabited him. This frequently forgotten place is his uncle's house on Roanoke Drive.

As readers are already aware from the earlier chapters of this book, many of the events related to the exorcism occurred at the house, which is still located today in the 8400 block of Roanoke Drive in Bel-Nor. The house, a picturesque brick structure, stands on a tree-lined block in this quiet St. Louis suburb. It is a quiet area and a place where it seems hard to believe that the terrifying events described in these pages could have occurred.

But in 1949, evil took up residence in this brick house.

In the fall of 2005, I learned that the house on Roanoke Drive had come up for sale. Eager to see the inside of the house that had been such a large part of my research for so many years, I eagerly contacted the realtor who had absolutely no interest in discussing the property with me. In fact, he was quite angry when I told him who I was and why I was interested in the house. He said that he was aware of the "supposed" connection the house had to the exorcism but that "none of that actually happened here, it was at a hospital." When I explained that this was not the case and began to tell him how much of the exorcism actually occurred in the house, he hung up on me. He did not return any of the other calls that I placed to his office.

The owner of the house, a real-estate investor who had never actually lived there, also claimed to have little knowledge about the exorcism. He said that he only became aware of the "rumors" after he purchased the house from a bankruptcy in the summer. The last person to occupy the house, Elvis Fantroy, abandoned the house in June 2005 and was never heard from again.

This rather ominous fact did not seem to bother Gary Stafford, the investor who purchased it a couple of months later. He said that he was not aware of the house being "haunted" or anything like that. "It's certainly not something we'd need to disclose to the future buyer," he said in an interview, "that, some 50 years ago, a boy who stayed in the house may or may not have been possessed. Besides, the exorcism didn't happen there."

The owner of the house seemed to be as unaware of the place's history as the real estate agent was but the same could not be said for the neighbors and residents of other homes on and near Roanoke Drive. Although I was unable to obtain a tour of the house, or an appointment with the realtor, I did visit the house in November 2005. The neighbors that I spoke with assured me that the fact that this was the "exorcism house" was one of the worst-kept secrets in the city.

"Everyone knows about it," I was told by one of them, "but there have never been any stories about bad things happening here."

My brief tour certainly didn't seem to suggest anything different. There was nothing about the house that chilled me, even with the knowledge that I have about what happened here in 1949. The place was silent and empty when I saw it and there was nothing out of place, save for a broken basement window. On the surface, there was nothing mysterious about the place that hearkened back to the weird events that occurred here but there is no question that it stands as a monument to one of the greatest unsolved mysteries in the history of America.

But that turned out not to be my final visit to the "Exorcism House" in Bel-Nor.

AFTERWORD:

Over the course of the last twenty-some years, I have been writing about and researching the unexplained, the unsolved and the supernatural. During that time, I have published more than one hundred books on these subjects and the original edition of *The Devil Came to St. Louis* was one of them. Prior to writing the book, I spent years researching the story of the 1949 exorcism, conducting interviews, visiting libraries and exploring buildings that were allegedly connected to the case. I spoke to scores of people involved, although only Father Walter Halloran was involved directly. After his death in 2005, the last true link to the case was broken. The story of the exorcism haunted me for years and even with all of the other books that I had written, I never forgot the details of the eerie, compelling story - or what happened to me during the course of writing it.

I have written about some pretty strange things during my career - ghosts, poltergeists, violent murders, depraved killers, cannibals, and worse. However, it was only during my work on the original edition of this book that the strange things that I was writing about seemed to find me. I often tell people that, sometimes, when you're writing about the unexplained, you become a part of the story, whether you want to or not. That's exactly what happened to me when I

168

was working on *The Devil Came to St. Louis.* During the winter of 2005-2006, when I was writing the book, weird things began to happen in my previously un-haunted house. All of them seemed to be connected to my writing the book. My notes disappeared, photographs vanished, recorded interviews mysteriously became garbled, items on my desk vanished and then turned up again in odd places and even large chunks of the book went missing, only to appear in different files on my computer.

Believe it or not, I have never been all that superstitious and my belief has always been that man created the so-called "devil" as an excuse for the horrible things that have happened throughout history. I have never claimed that Robbie Doe was possessed by a demon. I don't know - I can't even tell you exactly what demons are. On the other hand, though, I have always maintained that *something* happened in this case. I can't tell you what that *something* was, but I can say with great conviction that it was earthshaking enough that it caused an entire family to uproot itself and move halfway across the country to make it stop. Demons? Mental illness? Prank gone wrong? I can't tell you for sure, but it was terrifying. And it was *something*, there's no question about it.

I can also tell you that *something* happened in my house during the writing of this book. This was not my imagination at work or forgetfulness about where I left things on my desk. Weird stuff was going on and it was disturbing. I have never been quite so glad to finish a book.

Once those final pages were complete, I believed that my connection to the case was finally over. I had compiled my years of research into a narrative and exploration of what happened in St. Louis in 1949. Aside from book signings, interviews and an occasional presentation on the strange events, my version of the tale had been told.

And then I spent the night at the "Exorcism House."

For a number of years, while living in the St. Louis area, a great supporter of mine was popular radio show host, Dave Glover, who is still heard every afternoon on 97.1 THE TALK. I was frequently invited on the show by Dave and his producer, Tom Terbrock, to talk about ghosts and the unexplained and in particular, the St. Louis Exorcism. It was always a favorite topic of Dave's and we spent many on-the-air hours discussing the case. A huge part of the show has always been Dave's Halloween program, which was recorded and broadcast each October. Starting in the early 2000s, Dave took a few listeners chosen through a contest to a location in the St. Louis area to spend the night. I was always a fan of the show and provided background a few times for some of the locations.

Then, in 2008, I got a call from Tom about that season's Halloween show -
they would be recording it at the house in Bel-Nor where Robbie Doe's exorcism
had begun. I was no longer living in the St. Louis area, but was more than happy
to make the trip to help with the location recording. As readers recall, I had tried
to get a tour of the house a number of years before but had been turned away
by the realtor. The house had since been purchased by a private individual, but
he had offered it to Dave as a location for the Halloween show. As far as I was
concerned, the trip was worth the chance to see the interior of the house - notably
the bedroom where Robbie's exorcism had been started by Father Bowdern and
Father Bishop in 1949.

But keep in mind that, to me, this was just a historical spot - a curiosity that
played a large part in the history of the exorcism - and there was nothing scary
or spooky about it. I was thrilled to just be in the house where it all happened.

Or at least that's what I thought at the time.

When I arrived at the house in Bel-Nor on a warm October afternoon, I met
with Tom outside and we discussed the plans for the night. Three contestants
who had won the chance to visit the house on the radio show were being brought
to the house in blindfolds. They had no idea where they were being taken. After
they arrived, I was going to join Dave in detailing the history of the house and
the strange events that had taken place there. Once they were introduced to the
house - and the story of the exorcism - they would each spend one hour in the
bedroom where the exorcism took place. Needless to say, Dave and Tom were
hoping that they would be unsettled by the location.

Honestly, I had a tough time believing that would happen. As far as I was
concerned, it was just a house. Did something weird happen there? Absolutely.
But I didn't believe there was anything ghostly or strange still remaining at the
house. The exorcism had not even been completed there, I reasoned, so why would
anything remain behind?

At the time that I arrived, the crew was there, setting up equipment and gear
for the recording that night. Dave offered to show me around the house and I
readily agreed. I have to say that it was pretty amazing to get to stand in the
same rooms, walk the hallways and climb the stairs that had been used by the
exorcists and the family members of Robbie Doe sixty years before. After
walking around on the first floor, we climbed the stairs to the where the
bedrooms were located. At the top of the staircase, on the left side, was the
bedroom that Robbie had shared with his cousin - at least until the strange
happenings began. It was in that room where Father Bishop got his first look at
what he came to believe were diabolical events and where Father Bowdern began
trying to remove what he was convinced were demonic spirits from the young
boy's body.

To me, it was just a bedroom. It was certainly exciting for me to see. I had been reading, researching and writing about that room for more than fifteen years and it was pretty thrilling to see it, but in the end, it was just a room. But was it?

Dave walked into the room to show me around. There wasn't much to see. The new owner was in the midst of remodeling and the room had been stripped to the bare wood. The carpet had been removed and his footsteps rang out as he walked across the fairly small space. There was a closet on the far side of the room. On the left side of the doorway from where I stood had been the bed that Robbie had slept in - the same bed that Walter Halloran had seen lift several inches off the floor. Across from me were windows - the same windows that family members had opened to air out the room when noxious odors had overwhelmed them. In the center of the room was a single chair. The contestants would sit in the chair while they were spending their hour in what was visually a pretty uninteresting room. Again, there wasn't much to see.

For me, it was a bit of a letdown. After all of the years of hearing about the room, this was all there was to it. I was leaning against the doorframe, looking around, taking in the bare walls and wooden floor and wondering what the contestants would do in the room for an entire hour.

And then Dave invited me to come inside.

I started to put my foot forward and step into the room - and I froze. For whatever reason, it was impossible for me to walk forward. I was physically unable to move. I simply could not walk into the room. I knew - deep in my brain - that there was nothing out of the ordinary about this room. It was a simple room with a strange history, but just a room. So, what was wrong with me? Why couldn't I move?

I'm not exaggerating when I say that I literally could not walk inside. It was not my imagination at work either. I didn't believe that there was anything out of the ordinary about that room. My brain knew this fact - but it apparently had forgotten to pass that information along to my body. I was stuck in place for almost an entire minute before I could move. Dave invited me inside one more time and that seemed to break the spell. My feet lurched forward and I walked into the room.

And that's when the "feeling" overpowered me.

I have never claimed to have any sort of psychic ability. In fact, I am fond of telling people that "I'm as psychic as a fencepost." However, on that day and in that place, a terrible feeling of dread swept over me like nothing I have ever experienced before. It was a cold, sickening, almost electric feeling that came over me like a wave. I don't know where it came from, but I could feel it - and see it. I nudged Dave and held out my arm in front of me. Every hair on my arm was standing on end! It was like I had walked into an electrical current. I told him how strange I was feeling and in a matter of seconds, both of us walked out of the room, went downstairs and back outside. I was unnerved by what had happened to me - largely because I expected nothing out of the ordinary.

I had been researching the 1949 exorcism for years, but Dave had been fascinated with it for just as long. He is the first to admit that the story has scared him since he was a kid and he never gets tired of talking about it. He readily admitted that he was terrified to be at the house that night and claimed that he'd barely slept for the two weeks prior to the show taping. I think he was less surprised by what had happened in that bedroom than I was. And he would certainly turn out to be less surprised by the events that followed later that night.

Later that evening, a radio station van arrived at the house and brought the three contestants that were going to be spending the night in the house, each locked separately in Robbie's former bedroom upstairs. Once they arrived, Dave provided them with an introduction to the night, which included clips from *The Exorcist* on a big-screen television and a warning that he would be asking them to do something that night that he would never dare do himself. He told them, "This is not a haunted house, or some kind of spookshow. This is the Exorcist House. It's the real thing."

He then gave them a chance to back out and one of the contestants, Kelly, immediately burst into tears. "I can't do it," she sobbed. "I'm really sorry. I don't know what's wrong, this is so embarrassing. I don't even believe in this stuff. But the second I walked in this door.... Something really bad is going to happen. I can't stay here." After Kelly was calmed down, she was taken out of the house and she ended her participation for the night. This left the two other participants, Kristin and Matt, to experience the house on their own.

"There's something in that house," Kelly said before she left. "I can't be in there, or I'll just lose it."

Matt was the first of the remaining contestants to spend time in the upstairs bedroom. While he was inside, the rest of us vacated the house and went out to the detached garage, where there was recording and monitoring equipment set up. Everything that occurred in the bedroom would be recorded, although none of us would be able to hear it while it was taking place.

After it was over, we were able to hear what Matt had experienced. During his time in the room, he heard shuffling and scraping sounds in the room and out in the hallway. At first, he was convinced that someone was in the house with him it was empty and he frequently called out, but received no reply. At one point, the door handle to the room loudly rattled - so loudly that it could be heard on the recording. He was so sure that someone was outside the door, he pulled it

172

open - and then fled from the room when he found the hallway was empty. He left long before his hour was over.

Kristin did not last even as long as Matt did.

Dave escorted her to the room and she sat down in the chair, where she audibly recited the Lord's Prayer. Speaking aloud for the radio broadcast, she assured herself that she was in an ordinary room, in an ordinary house in a quiet neighborhood - but this did not stop her heart from beating so wildly that she began to shake uncontrollably. A shadow appeared under the doorway although, once again, the house was empty. Knocking sounds were heard in the hallway and inside the walls. And then when a thumping and dragging sound which can be heard on the recording loudly crashed outside of the door, Kristin began to scream for help, begging in a bloodcurdling voice for someone to come into the house and get her! Dave dashed up the stairs and into the room to find Kristin trembling, shaking and crying. She quickly recovered after he took her outside, but she refused to go back into the house. She had only been in the bedroom for eight minutes.

For those of us in the garage, we could hear nothing of what was taking place in the bedroom. We knew that Matt had come out after only a few minutes inside and that he had reported strange sounds, but little else. We waited anxiously while Kristin was in the room and then suddenly, we heard her terrible screams echo out of the room and throughout the dark neighborhood. We were lucky, I suppose, that none of the neighbors called the police, thinking that someone was being murdered. I couldn't help but think of what the neighbors in 1949 must have been thinking about the horrible sounds that they heard coming from the house next door as Robbie's exorcism was beginning.

It was a strange night and it was one that I'll never forget.

The night at the house in Bel-Nor ended in chaos, but it left an indelible impression on me - and honestly affected my opinion about what really happened in St. Louis in 1949. I still don't have a definitive opinion to offer on the validity of the possession, but I cannot help but think that there is real evil in the world and that sometimes, it leaves a physical presence behind. The case of Robbie Doe, whether you believe in possession, demons or exorcisms, remains unquestionably unsolved.

You may not believe that people can become diabolically possessed, but there is no way to adequately dismiss every unusual thing that happened in this case. As I have said many times, *something* happened to Robbie Doe, his family, scores of witnesses and a group of priests in 1949. What that *something* may have been remains a mystery - a mystery that none among us can easily solve.

173

BIBLIOGRAPHY & RECOMMENDED READING

Allen, Thomas B. - *Possessed*, 1993

Blatty, William Peter --- *William Peter Blatty on the Exorcist: From Novel to Film*, 1974

Brottman, Mikita --- *Hollywood Hex*, 1998

Courtaway, Robbi - *Spirits of St. Louis*, 1999

Ebon, Martin - *Demon Children*, 1978

---------------- - *The Devil's Bride*, 1974

---------------- - *Exorcism: Fact Not Fiction*, 1974

---------------- - *They Knew the Unknown*, 1971

Erdmann, Steve - "*The Truth Behind "The Exorcist*" - *Fate* Magazine; January 1975

Fate Magazine - March 1971

Fate Magazine --- October 1977

Fate Magazine - February 1990

Guiley, Rosemary Ellen - *Encyclopedia of Ghosts & Spirits*, 2000

Hill, Douglas & Pat Williams - *The Supernatural*, 1965

Kermode, Mark --- *The Exorcist*, 1997

Levack, Brian - *The Devil Within*, 2013

Linzee, David - *Infamous St. Louis Crimes & Mysteries*, 2001

Linson, D.R. - "*Washington's Haunted Boy*" - *Fate* Magazine; April 1951

Masters, Anthony - *The Devil's Dominion*, 1978

Melton, J. Gordon Editor *Encyclopedia of Occultism & Parapsychology*, 1996

Nicola, Rev. John J. --- *Diabolical Possession & Exorcism*, 1974

Opsasnick, Mark - *The Haunted Boy* - *Strange* Magazine; December 1998

Osterreich, Traugott - *Possession and Exorcism*, 1974

Riverfront Times Newspaper

Spencer, John & Anne - *The Poltergeist Phenomenon*, 1997
St. Louis Globe-Democrat Newspaper
St. Louis Post-Dispatch Newspaper
Strange Magazine 21 - Exorcist Case Update by Mark Chorvinsky
Taylor, Troy - *The Devil & All His Works*, 2012
---------------- - *The Devil Came to St. Louis*, 2006
---------------- - *Haunted St. Louis*, 2002
----------------- - *Sex & the Supernatural*, 2009
Travers, Peter   Stephanie Reiff --- *The Story Behind the Exorcist*, 1974
Wellesley, Gordon - *Sex & The Occult*, 1973
Wheatley, Dennis - *The Devil and All His Works*, 1973

Personal Interviews & Correspondence

Special Thanks to:
April Slaughter - Cover Design and Advice
Father Walter Halloran
Ray Nelke
Mark Chorvinsky
Dave Glover
Tom Terbrock
Corey Stulce
Len Adams
Bill Alsing
Lisa Taylor-Horton
Haven & Helayna Taylor

ABOUT THE AUTHOR: TROY TAYLOR

Troy Taylor is a writer, crime buff, supernatural historian and the author of more than 100 books on ghosts, hauntings, history, crime and the unexplained in America. He is also the founder of the American Hauntings Tour company. When not traveling to the far-flung reaches of the country in search of the unusual, Troy resides part-time in Decatur, Illinois.

See Troy's other titles at: **www.whitechapelpress.com**

CPSIA information can be obtained at www.ICGtesting.com
Printed in the USA
LVOW03s1139161015

458564LV00013B/110/P